D0713458

Produced by:
Quintessentially Publishing Ltd.
10 Carlisle Street
London W1D 3BR
Tel: +44 (0)845 388 1498
Fax: +44 (0)207 692 0213
www.quintessentiallypublishing.com

Design by:
Quintessentially Design Ltd.
Tel: +44 (0)20 7758 3331

ISBN: 978-0-9558270-9-9

QUINTESSENTIALLY RESERVE

We are thrilled to be bringing you the fifth edition of Quintessentially Reserve. From Scotland to New Zealand; from Canada to Russia, we have showcased the most exclusive luxury resorts, hotels, adventure lodges, safari camps and destinations imaginable on earth. So whether you're looking for a place to relax in the sun on a pristine beach, shop until you drop in a glamorous city, or trek in the wilderness we trust you will find something to suit everyone's taste within these pages.

We take great care in selecting the cream of the crop and identifying what we think matters most about each and every place – be it an intimate boutique hotel in Europe, a beachside hideaway in Asia, or a penthouse overlooking Central Park.

You can also seek additional advice from Quintessentially Travel which offers bespoke travel arrangements all over the world. To arrange stays at any of the addresses in this book, email qreserve@quintessentiallytravel.com or call +44 845 224 6915. Our experts will be happy to assist you.

I hope you'll enjoy this book as much as we enjoyed putting it together.

QUINTESSENTIALLY RESERVE – featuring 150 of the most sought-after and unique global travel destinations.
www.quintessentiallyreserve.com

QUINTESSENTIALLY PURE – a collection of 100 of the most beautiful spas in the world.
www.quintessentiallypure.com

QUINTESSENTIALLY LIVING – a stunning art book and directory of everything needed for the luxury home.
www.quintessentiallyliving.com

QUINTESSENTIALLY PERFUME – a beautiful insight into the world's most inspired, innovative and authentic perfumes.

QUBE – the social networking site for Quintessentially members and their friends.
www.qubers.com

QUINTESSENTIALLY PUBLISHING

WEBSITES
Websites

BRANDING
Branding

ONLINE MARKETING
Online Marketing

PACKAGING
Packaging

PRINT
Print

PHOTOGRAPHY
Photography

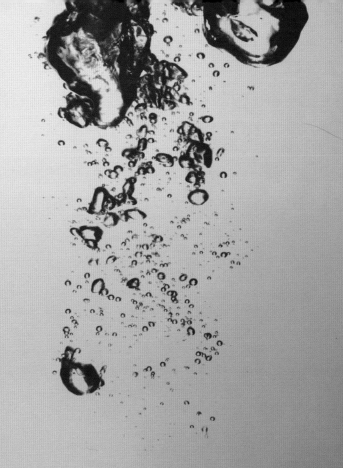

QUINTESSENTIALLY DESIGN
WWW.QUINTESSENTIALLYDESIGN.COM

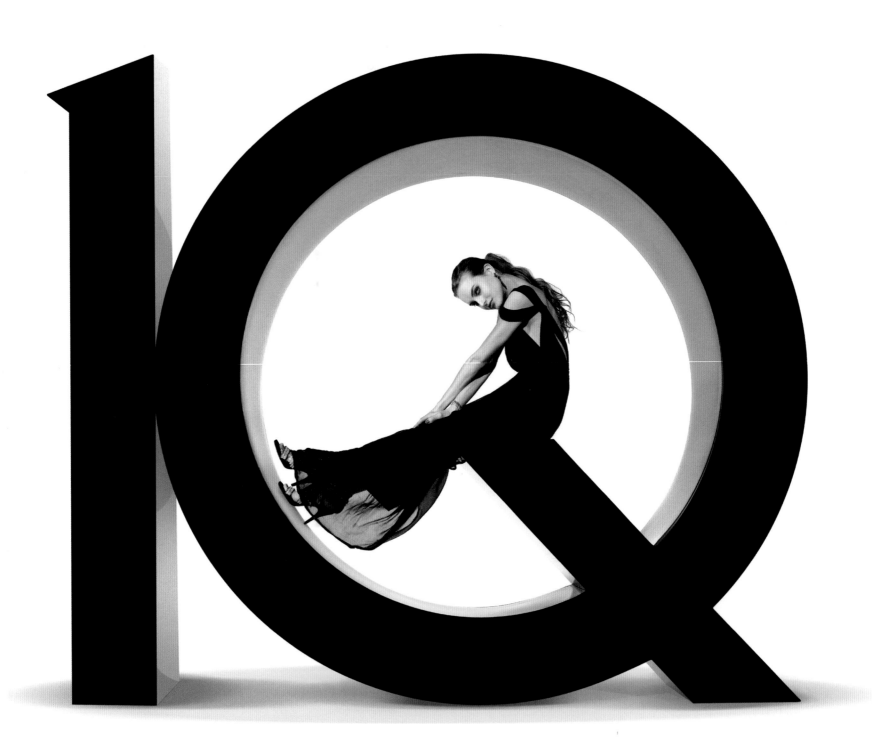

QUINTESSENTIALLY

Over the past 10 years, the Quintessentially Group has expanded exponentially from the UK's premier concierge service into a global luxury lifestyle empire, with over 60 offices and 32 sister businesses worldwide. Our unparalleled network of suppliers ensures members always receive exclusive access to the hottest VIP events, cultural happenings, top restaurants, spas and hotels – no matter where you are, no matter what time of day. Our sister businesses provide members with specialist luxury lifestyle offerings including: rare, fine wines; private jets, luxury cars and yachts; party planners; art consultants; property investment opportunities; bespoke gifting and styling services – and much more.

Put simply, our job is to provide Quintessentially Members with the very best that life has to offer.

Join today for immediate access.

membership@quintessentially.com | +44 (0)845 388 4329
www.quintessentially.com

Part of the Quintessentially Group
www.quintessentiallygroup

ABIDJAN | ABU DHABI | ABUJA | ACCRA | ALMATY | AMMAN | ATHENS | AUCKLAND | BAKU | BANGKOK | BARBADOS
BEIJING | BEIRUT | BOGOTÁ | BRUSSELS | BUENOS AIRES | CAIRO | CASABLANCA | COPENHAGEN | DUBAI | DUBLIN | GENEVA
HONG KONG | ISTANBUL | JEDDAH | JOHANNESBURG | KIEV | KUALA LUMPUR | KUWAIT CITY | LAGOS | LISBON | LONDON
LOS ANGELES | MANAMA | MAPUTO | MEXICO CITY | MIAMI | MILAN | MOSCOW | MUNICH | NAIROBI | NEW DELHI
NEW YORK | OSLO | PANAMA CITY | PARIS | PORT HARCOURT | PORT LOUIS | SAN FRANCISCO | SÃO PAULO | SEOUL
SHANGHAI | SINGAPORE | ST. JULIANS | STOCKHOLM | SYDNEY | TOKYO | TORONTO | VANCOUVER | VIENNA

Banyan Tree Vabbinfaru, Maldives

QUINTESSENTIALLY TRAVEL

A GLOBAL LUXURY TOUR OPERATOR OFFERING
UNFORGETTABLE TAILOR-MADE HOLIDAYS

Invites you to enjoy our exclusive travel services, opening up a world of uncompromising luxury and excellence.

We create tailor-made itineraries to some of the globe's most glamorous, sought-after and remote destinations; providing access to the most elegant and elite hotels, whilst offering value-for-money and unique travel experiences, with a service and benefits package unrivalled in the luxury travel market.

Having travelled from New York to New Delhi, Patagonia to the Philippines and everywhere in between, our international travel specialists are on hand 24 hours a day, 365 days a year to offer personalised care, unsurpassed global knowledge and impartial advice on the best destinations and accommodation to suit any request you might have.

To enquire about this exceptional service, please email
reserve@quintessentiallytravel.com or contact one of our travel specialists:

LONDON	NEW YORK	HONG KONG	JOHANNESBURG	DUBAI
+44 845 224 6915	+1 646 215 2167	+852 2540 8595	+27 11 911 4205	+971 44 376 802

www.quintessentiallytravel.com

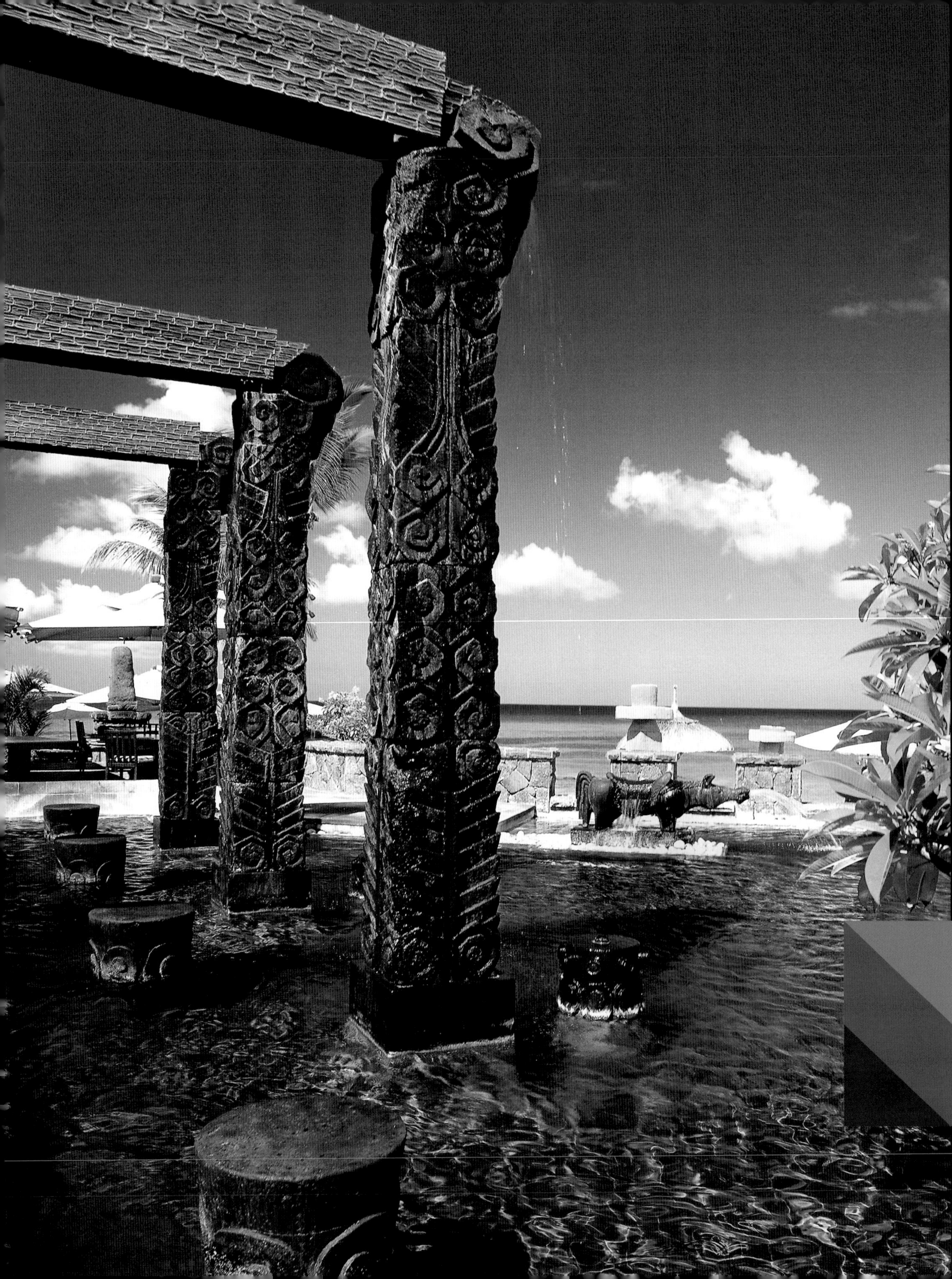

AFRICA & INDIAN OCEAN

SHANGRI-LA'S VILLINGILI RESORT & SPA

VILLINGILI ISLAND, MALDIVES.
COORDINATES – S 0° 40.528, E 73° 11.574

Shangri-La's Villingili Resort and Spa is the first luxury resort in the Maldives south of the equator. This is more impressive than just a geographical statistic. The property offers guests a stylish experience in a natural environment, the boutique-style resort encompassing lush vegetation including 17,000 coconut trees, four miles of picturesque coastline and over a mile of white sandy beach. Yet the journey is still straightforward: a 70-minute flight from Male international airport to Gan on Addu Atoll, then just an easy eight-minute speedboat ride to the resort. Accommodation ranges from private ocean retreats to tropical treehouse villas (unique to the Maldives) with panoramic views. The more adventuresome guest can explore by bicycle the five neighbouring islands and their rich Maldivian culture, connected by a 10 -mile road.

Q INSIDER: Addu Atoll's impressive reefs make this a popular area with scuba divers (the 140m 'British Loyalty' shipwreck is just a half-hour boat ride away). You can otherwise just hop on a bicycle and picnic beneath the palms, the resort allowing for that perfect mix of action and repose.

For booking enquiries contact Quintessentially Travel
Email: reserve@quintessentiallytravel.com, Tel: +44 (0)845 224 6915

NALADHU MALDIVES

SOUTH MALÉ ATOLL, MALDIVES
COORDINATES – N 03° 58.300, E 073° 30.391

On a tranquil palm-covered atoll surrounded by a coral lagoon Naladhu, meaning 'beautiful isle', offers simple seclusion within an easy 35-minute boat ride from the Maldives' international airport It is a place where everything is as it should be, each of Naladhu's 19, 300sq m beach and ocean houses with the feel of a private home rather than a Maldivian resort-hotel. Free-flowing spaces create a relaxed, light-filled spirit. All houses have an open-air bath steam room and garden rain shower, a private plunge pool, gardens multi-tiered hardwood deck and dining sala. Activities are relaxed from catamaran sailing to a private dinner on the beach. The idea is that you call the shots – a massage in your garden, a snorkeling excursion, a languid game of backgammon with drinks brought to your terrace.

Q INSIDER: Vanilla candles at bedtime. Your favourite jazz CD on the stereo. Each villa is allocated a House Master who is responsible for masterminding all the service details. He can even draw you a green tea bath. So be imaginative; as they say, you don't get if you don't ask.

For booking enquiries contact Quintessentially Travel
Email: reserve@quintessentiallytravel.com, Tel: +44 (0)845 224 6915

COA ISLAND

SOUTH MALE ATOLL, MALDIVES
COORDINATES – N 03° 55.072, E 073° 28.199

Cocoa Island, known locally as Makunufushi, allows guests to sink into the Maldives' quintessential spirit. It lies among South Male's coral, a 40-minute speedboat transfer from the international airport. Natural landscaping has not been interfered with, featuring palms, wild sea grapes, hibiscus and Maldivian Kajan. The house reef encloses a gin-clear lagoon that is rich with marine life, including rays and baby sharks. Each of the 33 rooms – which include eight Dhoni Suites, 10 Loft Villas and the spectacular COMO Villas – sit offshore on the southern side of the island, overhanging the lagoon. They are reached by planked walkways. Natural materials are carried through to the clean-lined, airy interiors, with high-raftered ceilings and glossy teak flooring. At Ufaa restaurant, menus display a rigorous reliance on well sourced, seasonal ingredients. Guests can also benefit from a holistic spa, COMO Shambhala Reterat, offering Yoga, facials and body treatments, as well as healthful COMO Shambhala Cuisine.

Q INSIDER: COMO Shambhala Retreat offers a series of 'Paths for Wellness' comprising suggested treatments (from 150 minutes to six hours long) to help better the mind-body balance. They include The Purification Path, Relaxation Path, Rejuvenation Path and Restoration Path.

For booking enquiries contact Quintessentially Travel
Email: reserve@quintessentiallytravel.com, Tel: +44 (0)845 224 6915

BAROS MALDIVES

BAROS, MALDIVES. COORDINATES – N 4° 17.087, E 73° 25.631

Even with the turquoise, reef-ringed, white-sand shores for which this archipelago is known, Baros Maldives stands apart from the crowd. Much of this is to with the rich tropical landscaping of this private island's lush, flower-filled interior, with villas set among sunny glades (all 24 of the Deluxe-level rooms have their own walled garden). The 103sq m Baros Villas (10 units) are paces from the beach while the 30 Water Villas (92sq m) occupy a peaceful, crescent-shaped place of their own reached by a short boardwalk stretching over the water. This is a property that prides itself on delivering the luxury experience from start to finish (private 25-minute speedboat transfers from Male international airport), and top to bottom (no kids under eight help to maintain the resort's serene feel). There are two restaurants to choose from for dinner, two bars, and a dedicated dive instruction team on site.

Q INSIDER: To have both your own private pool and the lagoon waters on hand is spoiling indeed. At Baros Maldives, there are 10 villas with this abundance of riches. In addition the resort's 268sq m Baros Residence, with round-the-clock butler services, has the largest pool of all set amidst the ferns and bird-of-paradise blooms.

For booking enquiries contact Quintessentially Travel
Email: reserve@quintessentiallytravel.com, Tel: +44 (0)843 224 6915

VELASSARU MALDIVES

SOUTH MALE ATOLL, MALDIVES.
COORDINATES – N 04° 07.275, E 073° 26.212

Velassaru Maldives - an easy 25-minute speedboat journey from Male's airport – sits on a private coral island with the archipelago's signature white sands and turquoise sea. Stunning water and beach villas are designed in thatch, stone and teak – architecture which is matched by the seaview spa and infinity pool. There is a remarkable choice in dining options, with no less than five restaurants offering different notes in world cuisine from Asian to Mediterranean to a traditional Japanese grill serving contemporary Japanese sushi and teppanyaki dishes. Activities on the offer don't only include the obvious Maldives' bestsellers – snorkeling and diving – but there is also a tennis court and gym. The feel throughout is youthful and contemporary, with overwater deck areas to rooms so guests feel as if they are the only people on earth.

Q INSIDER: The overwater spa has 10 treatment pavilions set on stilts – a contemporary design instilled with Maldivian flair to provide possibly the most relaxing environment imaginable for melting beneath the hands of one of Velassaru's expert therapists.

For booking enquiries contact Quintessentially Travel
Email: reserve@quintessentiallytravel.com, Tel: +44 (0)845 224 6915

MARADIVA
VILLAS RESORT & SPA

WOLMAR, MAURITIUS. COORDINATES – S 20° 17.008, E 57° 21.992

When Mark Twain visited Mauritius, he wrote that this small volcanic speck off the coast of Madagascar was Heaven's prototype. And this was before room service and private plunge pools. It seems Eden keeps getting better – not least with the presence of Maradiva Villas Resort & Spa. Set in 27 acres of lush tropical gardens on the island's west coast, the resort has its own beachfront. There are 65 suite villas (measuring 163 to 345 square metres each) – all of them colonial-style, with wood-carved façades, private pools and butler service. Some of the villas interconnect, making this a good choice for families (there is an impressive kids club, too, for children aged four to 12). The beach is that bristling white for which Mauritius is adored. But this isn't all. On an island where gourmet competition is steep, expect to enjoy a global spread of cuisines including Japanese, Thai, Vietnamese, Indian, Mediterranean and Mauritian specialties.

Q INSIDER: From Europe, the jet lag isn't killer. So you can't use sleep deprivation as an excuse for hanging out all day on a sun lounger. It is a must to explore this magical island's rich interior thick with mountains and sugar plantations – and to learn about the dodo.

For booking enquiries contact Quintessentially Travel
Email: reserve@quintessentiallytravel.com, Tel: +44 (0)845 224 6915

SHANTI MAURICE, A NIRA RESORT

CHEMIN GRENIER, MAURICE. – S 20° 30.352, E 57° 27.926

Shanti Maurice, a Nira Resort, is positioned between two versions of paradise. In front of the pristine horseshoe coral sand cove lie the bright blues of the Indian Ocean; behind rise the vivid greens of the sugarcane fields that give Mauritius its unique, tropical flavour. Shanti Maurice makes the most of this untouched, south coast location with a resort that's neither too large to dominate nor too small to be forgotten. Most significantly, the tenor is Mauritian through and through. With 61 rooms and suites and 17 villas with pools, the resort has an intimate feel, allowing every guest the space to connect with the island's sights, sounds and flavours of its mixed Indian, African, French and Chinese heritage. Guests can swim with dolphins at Tamarind Bay, or spend a leisurely lunch at Le Saint Aubin, a plantation house built in 1819. The extensive Nira Spa at Shanti Maurice – organic, using African botanicals – is built around an enchanting tea pavilion, the relaxing, purposeful treatments perfectly complementing the location as well as the traditional Ayurvedic programmes.

Q INSIDER: Shanti Maurice means to make itself heard with its contemporary Cape cooking as well as a second restaurant serving authentic Mauritian dishes. The resort has developed its own tasty wellness cuisine. There is also a beachside Fish and Rhum Shack for foot-in-the-sand dining.

For booking enquiries contact Quintessentially Travel
Email: reserve@quintessentiallytravel.com, Tel: +44 (0)845 224 6915

THE OBEROI MAURITIUS

POINTE AUX PIMENTS, MAURITIUS
COORDINATES – S 20° 04.551, E 057° 30.799

With Indian roots to Mauritius, it made sense for Oberoi to enter the fray on this spectacular Indian Ocean island. The company knows a thing or two about bringing local culture into their resort projects, from cuisine to spa treatments to the overall aesthetic. The property is located on the less developed northwest coast of Mauritius which tends to get more sun and less wind than elsewhere on the island from May to September. Nestled in the Baie aux Tortues, you are 15 minutes' drive from Port Louis, the capital. With only 71 rooms including 23 villas, the resort has an amazing landscape of fauna and flora amidst 20 acres of land. Most of the villas have private swimming pools. There are three restaurants serving French Mediterranean, Indian and Mauritian cuisines. The award-winning Oberoi Spa features Ayurveda and Africology treatments as well as complimentary sessions in hatha yoga, tai chi and sound meditation.

Q INSIDER: To discover the island of Mauritius, take part in the resort's complimentary 'Touching Senses' programme, which includes astronomy, a cooking demonstration, wine-tasting, and a local nature walk.

For booking enquiries contact Quintessentially Travel
Email: reserve@quintessentiallytravel.com, Tel: +44 (0)845 224 6915

BANYAN TREE
SEYCHELLES

MAHE, SEYCHELLES. COORDINATES – S 04° 46.929, E 055° 29.848

Mahe, the main island of the Seychelles, is enjoying a moment right now – and rightly so, for there are few places left that have beaches this unspoiled, with low-slung palms casting shadows over empty sands. Of the high-end resorts, Banyan Tree Seychelles stands as one of the originals – opened in 2002 when it secured the stellar location in scenic Intendance Bay. This resort is all about space, the 60 pool villas perched behind the beach and above, nestled in hilly terrain amid exotic flora and fauna. The design combines the best of Seychellois architecture – and contemporary, colonial and plantation décor – from high sloping ceilings to airy verandahs. Every villa features its own private infinity pool, as well as spacious living and dining pavilions. Then there is the award-winning spa (a Banyan signature) and the panoply of restaurants: Saffron for Thai food, Au Jardin D'Epices for international favourites and Chez Lamar for tastes of the Creole culture.

Q INSIDER: Surprise your travelling companion with the 'Harmony Banyan' – a three-hour spa session performed by two therapists in one of the eight hillside, ocean-facing spa cottages.

For booking enquiries contact Quintessentially Travel
Email: reserve@quintessentiallytravel.com, Tel: +44 (0)845 224 6915

RAFFLES PRASLIN, SEYCHELLES

PRASLIN, SEYCHELLES. COORDINATES – S 4° 18.313, E 55° 42.993

When it opens in February 2011, Raffles Praslin, Seychelles, intends to make a very loud noise in the luxury marketplace. For this is paradise layered as thick as the perfect mille-feuille, the resort positioned on a sugar-coated, dust-white beach stretching for some 500 metres. There are 86 elegantly appointed villas – none smaller than 125 square metres – complemented with the signature round-the-clock Raffles butler service. Every room has views of the Indian Ocean, lush greenery and those spectacular granite formations that make the Seychelles unique. The resort itself spreads over 30 hectares on the tranquil island of Praslin. The gourmet experience isn't just about the five restaurants and bars; dining ranges from picnics on sandbanks, to romantic dinners on the beach, in the garden, aboard a yacht or in your villa.

Q INSIDER: Nature lovers rave about the Vallée de Mai Nature Reserve. A UNESCO World Heritage site, its palm forests dotted with the Coco de Mer shelter some of the rarest creatures on earth such as the beautiful Seychelles Black Parrot and a myriad of wonderful reptiles, mammals and crustaceans.

For booking enquiries contact Quintessentially Travel
Email: reserve@quintessentiallytravel.com, Tel: +44 (0)845 224 6915

NORTH ISLAND

MAHE, SEYCHELLES. COORDINATES – S 04° 37.863, E 055° 26.095

North Island isn't just one of the world's most exclusive private island retreats. It is also a 'Noah's Ark', the perfect example of conservation meets high-end tourism. The accommodation – 11 breezy, well-spaced villas – displays a respect for context and style, combining driftwood with shells, rock and palm thatch. Yet there's nothing Flintstone about the finished look; the architects, also responsible for Tanzania's Ngorongoro Crater Lodge, are too fashion-forward to fall for that one. Cuisine is organic and locally sourced, reflecting the region's mixed heritage (from Southern Indian to African). There's scuba diving, snorkeling, sea kayaking, cycling, deep-sea fishing and island hopping, and a stunningly dramatic spa and rim-flow pool built into the rocks. The pièce de resistance (make that three) is the sand – white, powder-soft, clichés of Eden.

Q INSIDER: Villa 11 is built into the incline of the island's principal Anse d'Est Beach. Book it and you will get a bird's eye view of the sand, water and palms. Not that much goes on in these far-out waters. The point is the privacy and solitude.

For booking enquiries contact Quintessentially Travel
Email: reserve@quintessentiallytravel.com, Tel: +44 (0)845 224 6915

ROYAL MANSOUR
MARRAKECH

MARRAKECH, MOROCCO. COORDINATES – N 31° 37.634, W 8° 0.013

Royal Mansour Marrakech is the talk of all Morocco – an extraordinary new hotel mad up of 53 'private' riads (the traditional townhouse built around a central courtyard) Ranging from one to four bedrooms, each has its own butler, plunge pool and roo terrace looking out over the city's rooftops towards the distant Atlas. The larger riad also boast galleries and dining rooms with bars. There are three restaurants oversee by the three-star chef of Le Meurice in Paris, Yannick Alléno, as well as a vast 2500sc m spa. All this set in close to four hectares of manicured gardens inside the city's ol walls, meaning you're within an easy walk of the souks and the magic men that give this pink city its alluring power. But while the stats are impressive, it's the detail tha makes the difference, the meticulous design authentically representing the classic skill of Moroccan artisans.

Q INSIDER: No need to opt for an out-of-town resort anymore. Here you get all th same advantages and more, including an outdoor swimming pool, a children's clul complimentary WiFi in all public areas, beauty, fitness and gym facilities as well as pool in the spa area under a glazed pavilion.

For booking enquiries contact Quintessentially Travel
Email: reserve@quintessentiallytravel.com, Tel: +44 (0)845 224 6915

AMANJENA

MARRAKECH, MOROCCO. COORDINATES – N 31° 37.639, W 8° 0.014

When Amanjena arrived in Marrakech, it raised the game for this fashionable North African city. Travellers no longer had to contend with cramped riad hotels in the medina (the old town) but could luxuriate in this 39-suite property on the city's fringe – air-conditioned in summer, open fireplaces in winter. Service standards soared, for this is a place defined by its personalised approach, ranging from private dinners in caidal tents to a desert trip to the Sahara. There is no dress code, no opening times, and no chits to sign until you leave. Inspired by local palaces, the resort's walls are a sun-baked pink and grounds feature vast bassins (ornamental irrigation pools), domed pavilions and regal rose gardens. Space isn't at a premium here, with every suite free-standing. The Thai restaurant attracts the city's knowing ex-pats, and the health and beauty centre has a traditional hammam.

Q INSIDER: The top suite is the Al-Hamra Maison with two bedrooms, a private butler and 36sq metre heated pool. Alternatively, Q holds a flame for the six two-storey maisons – a notch down, but also two bedrooms each with a courtyard and pool. The bathtubs are a delicious green marble.

For booking enquiries contact Quintessentially Travel
Email: reserve@quintessentiallytravel.com, Tel: +44 (0)845 224 6915

KASBAH DU TOUBKAL

MARRAKECH, MOROCCO
COORDINATES – N 31° 14.999, W 007° 58.971

Kasbah du Toubkal belongs to a particular, passionate vision – an extraordinary venture an hour's drive from Marrakech in the Atlas Mountains, conceived as an imaginative partnership between Discover Ltd and the local Berber villagers. It's easy to see why this stunning hideaway has been recognised for its contributions to sustainable tourism – it employs local inhabitants and deploys energy-friendly under-floor heating in some of its 14 rooms. Families can enjoy the space offered with three interconnecting rooms and for those unable to escape their work duties, there is a small conference room and Wi-Fi access available. The views are the most breathtaking in North Africa with Toubkal, Morocco's highest mountain, rising up as spectacular backdrop to the hotel. No surprise then, that Martin Scorsese used it as a set for his film, Kundun, on the Dalai Lama. From the hotel you can take a leisurely stroll into the village of Imlil for a cup of mint tea, or just stay put, enjoying possibly the finest tagines in Morocco as well as authentic service and a warming hammam.

Q INSIDER: For a longer trek, each couple gets their own personal mountain guide, a mule and muleteer for luggage and at the end of the day, a warm bed and delicious food served up at the remote trekking lodge, a satellite four-bedroom lodge in the Azzeden Valley.

For booking enquiries contact Quintessentially Travel
Email: reserve@quintessentiallytravel.com, Tel: +44 (0)845 224 6915

BILILA LODGE

SERENGETI, TANZANIA. COORDINATES – S 02° 14.027, E 034° 55.127

Opened in July 2009, Bilila Lodge Kempinski brings a whole different style of luxury to the Serengeti – and in a part of Africa better known for canvas lodges. With 77 guest rooms including suites and five private villas – each of which boasts a stunning private swimming pool and butler service – guests can relax and be treated like royalty from the comfort of their own private paradise. This is among the largest full-service five-stars in Tanzania, all rooms overlooking the plains over which tens of thousands of wildebeest migrate when the rains start each November. If that annual spectacle isn't awe-inspiring enough, all rooms include luxury en-suite bathrooms, walk-in closets, and a sun deck for relaxation with a personal telescope for game watching. Suites have private plunge pools. There's an Anantara Spa with six double treatment rooms, three Thai massage rooms, a 24m infinity freshwater pool overlooking the waterhole, a restaurant, bar, lobby lounge, wine cellar, library, game room, fitness centre, gift and jewellery shop. The resort will take you out to explore the northern part of the National Park – an untouched area where it's just you, the ranger and the animals.

Q INSIDER: While it's everyone's hope and dream they'll feel the earth move with those thundering hooves, Bilila Lodge Kempinski is more than just a base for game viewing. With so much to occupy your time at the resort, Q recommends at least a five-night stay taking one of the lavish private Villas.

For booking enquiries contact Quintessentially Travel
email: reserve@quintessentiallytravel.com, Tel: +44 (0)845 224 6915

34

&BEYOND MNEMBA
ISLAND LODGE

MNEMBA ISLAND, ZANZIBAR. COORDINATES – S 05° 49.249, E 039° 23.004

&Beyond Mnemba Island Lodge is an Indian Ocean, private island paradise construed to feel unpretentious, effortless and aesthetically true to its locale. Ten rustic palm-frond bandas are tucked away in a tropical forest fringed by a white coral sand beach. A covered walkway leads to a shuttered ensuite bathroom with a huge glass-beaded shower. Zanzibar is famous for its intricate, detailed woodcarvings and the scrolled headboards adorning the beds are created by some of the island's most skilled artisans. Built-in 'barazas' on the verandah are perfect for afternoon siestas, and private beach salas feature traditional Zanzibari loungers for hanging out in the shade. Thatched dining areas have beautiful open views of the beach and spectacular vistas of Zanzibar beyond. Baskets of fresh fruit, fish, lobsters, crabs and prawns are sailed into Mnemba daily on traditional ngalawa outriggers, lunch often served on large wooden carved Zanzibar platters heaped with delicious mezze. In short, a better honeymoon retreat is hard to imagine.

Q INSIDER: Turtle season occurs between April and August (however layings can happen year round). Within nine weeks, Mnemba's sands are filled with tiny hatchlings. If you miss this phenomenal natural event, then snorkeling and diving these coral seas makes for an equally exciting marine adventure.

For booking enquiries contact Quintessentially Travel
Email: reserve@quintessentiallytravel.com, Tel: +44 (0)845 224 6915

LION SANDS
PRIVATE GAME RESERVE

SABI SAND GAME RESERVE, SOUTH AFRICA
COORDINATES – S 24° 42.528, E 031° 33.582

Lion Sands Private Game Reserve, family owned and managed since 1993, occupie
some of the world's finest wildlife territory; the property stretches for miles along the
Sabie River, which forms its natural boundary with South Africa's Kruger National Park
There are three different lodges: Lion Sands River Lodge (recently renovated to the tune
of $2million), Lion Sands Ivory Lodge (the jewel in the collection, run more like private
villas) and Lion Sands 1933. In addition to this, Lion Sands manages and operates two
lodges within the Kruger National Park, Tinga Legends and Tinga Narina, allowing
guests to experience both aspects of the Sabi Sand as well as the Kruger National Park
Each of the lodges has their own unique style and experience, with the two Kruger
lodges offering wellness treatments with professional health and skin care therapists
library with an array of African literature, traditional boma, lounge bar. All safaris ar
conducted by experienced professional guides.

Q INSIDER: Lion Sands offers guests an opportunity to sleep out in a Tree House, the
only one of its kind within the Sabi Sand Private Game Reserve.

For booking enquiries contact Quintessentially Travel
Email: reserve@quintessentiallytravel.com, Tel: +44 (0)845 224 6915

ROYAL MALEWANE

HOEDSPRUIT, SOUTH AFRICA. COORDINATES – S 24° 32.496, E 031° 02.288

Royal Malewane is safari with style, owned and designed by Liz Biden, South Africa's answer to all things glam. Not only have you got the Big Five in abundance – as the lodge is situated on a 30,000-acre reserve in the Greater Kruger region – but expect a swanky 10 stars in terms of luxury accommodation. A hub of linked walkways run between the Royal and Malewane suites on the extremities of the lodge (both with a private chef, a private vehicle, and able to accommodate families) and the six luxury rooms – each with its own wooden deck, rim-flow pool and thatched gazebo. The central area of the lodge (with a library, shop, viewing deck and wine cellar) fall under a canopy of indigenous acacia trees and plays setting for the wonderful combinations of Mediterranean and fusion dishes to be served. The Bush Spa – 'The Waters of Royal Malewane' – offers a magnitude of African – themed treatments. Facilities include indoor and outdoor therapy areas, a state-of-the-art gym, vichy shower, a health bar and a 25 m heated lap pool. Not bad for the wilderness.

Q INSIDER: In any other part of the world, the accommodation would suffice for a top-flight vacation. Here, you can add in fabulous game drives and expert rangers as well as six-course fine dining evenings with crystal glasses and a wide selection of top-class South African wines.

For booking enquiries contact Quintessentially Travel
Email: reserve@quintessentiallytravel.com, Tel: +44 (0)845 224 6915

MOLORI SAFARI LODGE

NIETVERDIEND, SOUTH AFRICA
COORDINATES – S 24° 43.205, E 026° 22.826

The word 'molori' means 'to dream' in the local language, which is exactly how it feels to stay at Molori Safari Lodge in South Africa. Anything but a typical safari camp, this luxury retreat is set within malaria-free Madikwe Game Reserve, a 50-minute flight from Johannesburg or a short heli transfer. Molori's warmth, charm and comfort reign supreme in the five meticulous open-air suites – an intimate size ideal for exclusive use; booked room by room, however, and you will feel like the only guests in the world, such is the sense of privacy nurtured by Molori's service ethic (36 staff to just five suites). Accommodations range from 232 to 619 square metres each; some are split-level, the two-bedroom format ideal for families. The presidential Metsi and Molelo Suites feature 24-hour butlering, one or two dining areas, a service kitchen, spacious lounge, walk-in closet, rim-flow bath, an outdoor shower, private infinity pool, Jacuzzi, library/study equipped with laptop, satellite flatscreen TV and DVD.

Q INSIDER: Apart from excellent game viewing, Molori offers culinary classes, star gazing, use of the fitness centre, same-day laundry and for a small extra cost – VIP airport handling. You get the drift, with in-room amenities including fully loaded iPods, Bose docking stations, espresso machines, wireless Internet and air-conditioning.

For booking enquiries contact Quintessentially Travel
Email: reserve@quintessentiallytravel.com, Tel: +44 (0)845 224 6915

TINTSWALO ATLANTIC

CAPE TOWN, SOUTH AFRICA
COORDINATES – S 34° 03.494, E 018° 22.055

Nestled within the boundaries of Table Mountain National Park and flanked by two world-renowned landmarks – the majestic Table Mountain and legendary Cape of Good Hope – lies Tintswalo Atlantic. Stylish yet understated, this new hotel offers home-away-from-home comforts, discreet service and mouth-watering culinary creations in a heart-stopping setting with ocean views. Explore the many paths and walkways within the Table Mountain National Park, which is known for its extraordinary fauna and flora; or stroll along the tranquil and secluded pebble beach. Enjoy lunch on the deck, share cooking tips with the executive chef in the open-plan kitchen, ending the day with an intimate dinner as the sun sets behind the Sentinel. For Cape Town, the experience doesn't get much more quintessential.

Q INSIDER: With 10 luxury suites and one regal presidential suite individually decorated according to a particular island's inspiration, Tintswalo Atlantic is one-of-a-kind; it is also the perfect size for an exclusive use buy-out.

For booking enquiries contact Quintessentially Travel
Email: reserve@quintessentiallytravel.com, Tel: +44 (0)845 224 6915

MORUKURU

MADIKWE GAME RESERVE. SOUTH AFRICA
COORDINATES – S 24° 45.611, E 26° 16.690

The Madikwe Reserve in game-rich South Africa is the location for the unique 'Morukuru Family' experience. In terms of bricks and mortar, or teak and thatch, you've got the Owner's House, Lodge and Farm House, with each of the villas (as they are called) operating on an exclusive basis. In other words, there are never any other guests beside you and those you choose to accompany you. The safaris are entirely private, led by your personal game ranger who works with a gifted Shangaan tracker. Other off-the-cuff adventures might include a romantic starlit sleepover at the double-storey bird hide, bush breakfasts, pizza picnics, candle-lit dinners and memorable barbecues beside the Marico River. Malaria-free and easily accessed out of Johannesburg (a short 50-minute journey on your own private 'Morukuru Air Charter Flight'), this is the 'big five safari' made easy.

Q INSIDER: For a safari experience, Morukuru doesn't come much more kid friendly, with the family-owned property understanding what visiting children want and need. Nannies, safe safaris, swimming, fishing and much more besides are laid on for guests

CAPE GRACE

CAPE TOWN, SOUTH AFRICA
COORDINATES – S 33° 54.515, E 018° 25.233

In Cape Town, escape the hustle by retreating to Cape Grace on the V&A Waterfront. On one side you've got the activity of the working harbour; on the other, the international yacht marina. Behind lies Signal Hill and Table Mountain. Cape Grace is located on a private quay and is defined by quietly efficient service. All 120 of the refashioned, Cape-influenced guestrooms and suites have French doors that open up to tranquil maritime views. Detail is homely, including mini-delis and iPod docking stations in every room. The rooftop spa offers African-inspired massages and aloe vera hydrotherapy facials. The hotel's Signal restaurant offers a vibrant combination of relaxed atmosphere, seamless service and adventurous culinary flair with modern South African influences. Cape Grace also has a fabulous library and heated outdoor pool with trellised gardens.

Q INSIDER: Younger guests are treated to African story-time and gingerbread decorating each evening, leaving mum and dad free to enjoy the complimentary Cape Orientation and Wine Tasting. For true romantic indulgence, opt for a sunset cruise with a private wine or whisky tasting on board Cape Grace's luxury yacht, 'Spirit of the Cape'. Perfection.

For booking enquiries contact Quintessentially Travel
Email: reserve@quintessentiallytravel.com, Tel: +44 (0)845 224 6915

EMIRATES PALACE

ABU DHABI, UNITED ARAB EMIRATES. COORDINATES – N 24° 27.657, E 054° 19.030

Emirates Palace claims to be the most expensive hotel ever built – an extravagance in gold, silver and mother of pearl. Traditional palatial architecture – adorned with exquisite silk and Persian carpets and handpicked crystal chandeliers – is meshed with modern day technology; this includes the fastest WiFi connectivity in the UAE, which envelops the entire 100 hectares including the mile-long private beach. There's an Anantara Spa, tennis courts, Sarab Land kids club and a FIFA-approved world-class soccer pitch. All rooms and suites have butler service to fulfill your whims. Accommodation also features private balconies or terraces overlooking the palatial gardens or the Arabian Gulf. Pampering the palate is a Picasso-esque art of colour and expression; the array of cuisines includes modern Cantonese (Hakkasan), Pacific Rim, Mediterranean, Persian, Italian and Lebanese and the first Emirati five-star restaurant in UAE serving local and traditional cuisine (Mezlai).

Q INSIDER: The family-friendly adventure pool has slides and waterfalls. The relaxation pool promises pure serenity with numerous Jacuzzis and a bar serving delectable drinks. Whatever your purpose – honeymoon, business, winter

BURJ AL ARAB

DUBAI, UNITED ARAB EMIRATES. COORDINATES – N 25° 08.464, E 055° 11.128

Burj Al Arab is more than a super-luxe hotel; it is a landmark for the new Dubai. Fashioned after the billowing sail of an Arabian dhow, it soars up to 321 metres, occupying a man-made island 280 metres off Jumeirah Beach. All suites are duplex and have floor-to-ceiling windows that command glittering Gulf views. Most suites are bedecked in gold with the headline accommodation displaying a panoply of colours (check out The Royal Suite with its richly ornamented interior scheme and revolving four – poster bed). Q loves the full-size Hermes bathroom amenities and the brigade of butlers. The aquarium-style Al Mahara restaurant matches the standard set by its unique style with perfect seafood (there are six other eateries, as well as Skyview Bar). The Assawan Spa & Health Club offers every conceivable luxury including an 85-minute 'Around the World' massage (Shiatsu, Balinese, Swedish, Thai….)

Q INSIDER: Try out Junsui, the hotel's new Asian restaurant. With 12 live stations and 45 specialised Asian chefs, Junsui offers a mouth-watering union of culinary delights from Japan, China, Indonesia, Thailand and Korea. You also have breathtaking views over the Arabian Gulf.

ARMANI HOTEL DUBAI

DUBAI, UNITED ARAB EMIRATES
COORDINATES – N 25° 11.836, E 055° 16.469

Soaring high above Downtown Dubai in the iconic Burj Khalifa, the world's tallest tower, and within walking distance of the world's largest mall, The Dubai Mall, the Armani Hotel Dubai is the first hotel designed and developed by Giorgio Armani. Reflecting the elegance simplicity and sophisticated comfort that define Armani's signature style, the hotel is the realisation of the designer's long-held dream to offer his customers a 'Stay with Armani' experience. Every detail in the hotel bears the designer's style features, from the warm Italian style hospitality and stunning Eramosa stone floors, to the bespoke furnishings and personally designed hotel amenities. Refined colours clean lines and unique textures blend seamlessly with the tower's impressive architecture and natural light creating a serene atmosphere throughout. There are eight restaurants ranging from Japanese and Indian to Mediterranean and authentic Italian cuisine. The Armani Ballroom, Pavilion, Al Majlis and meeting rooms are perfect for hosting business events while the spa is a 12,000 sq ft oasis of peace and tranquility in the heart of a bustling city.

Q Insider: For the ultimate in pampering and tailor-made experiences your very own 'Lifestyle Manager' can help you chart out an itinerary plan your stay and is there to welcome you the minute you step into the hotel.

For booking enquiries contact Quintessentially Travel
Email: reserve@quintessentiallytravel.com, Tel: +44 (0)845 224 6915

RAFFLES DUBAI

DUBAI, UNITED ARAB EMIRATES
COORDINATES – N 25° 13.675, E 055° 19.224

Raffles Dubai, inspired by the great pyramids of Egypt, is an iconic 19-storey pyramidal structure with a pre-eminent position in the landscape of this über-modern Middle Eastern city. For opulence, the hotel interiors are hard to beat, each of the 246 rooms and suites of palatial size with terraces offering breathtaking urban views. With a city centre location, this hotel is great for shoppers drawn to Dubai's many super-malls; in fact, to visit Wafi Mall, Dubai's premium lifestyle complex, guests of Raffles Dubai need only walk an air-conditioned corridor. There are eight restaurants and bars, with the award-winning Noble House located at the peak of the pyramid. The lively evening vibe centres around RED Lounge and Terrace, and Crystal nightclub. For the morning after, a visit to Raffles Amrita Spa wouldn't go amiss. Then either take a relaxing dip in the pool or take your Thesiger to read in the shade of the Raffles Botanical Garden – an enchanting one-hectare haven in central Dubai, planted with 129,000 plant species.

Q INSIDER: Make time for a visit to the city's gold souk, calling upon the highly trained Raffles concierge for the inside track on what to pay, where to buy and who to trust. There is a gravitas to this very old, culturally layered city (a history often forgotten with the buzz of the new).

For booking enquiries contact Quintessentially Travel
Email: reserve@quintessentiallytravel.com, Tel: +44 (0)845 224 6915

W DOHA HOTEL & RESIDENCES

DOHA, QATAR. COORDINATES – N 25° 19.653, E 051° 31.719

W Doha Hotel & Residences encapsulates a casual urban vibe while also hitting all the notes for oil-rich Qataris. Just take a look at the credentials. There are two concept restaurants from Jean-Georges Vongerichten, as well as a temple to the black stuff – La Maison du Caviar – and a sparkling Crystal Lounge boasting a Baccarat centrepiece. You can do business nearby, for the hotel is positioned in the heart of West Bay only a breath away from the City Centre Shopping Mall and Doha's major corporate towers. But it is during your downtime when this hotel really comes into its own, with an outdoor Wet® swimming pool, a Sweat Fitness® Center, and a sybaritic Bliss® Spa, all 60 guest rooms, 42 suites and 138 W Branded Residences contemporary fiefdoms unto themselves. So spread out, live large and bring your entourage – pausing to take in those breathtaking Arabian Gulf views.

Q INSIDER: Under W brand's signature Whatever/Whenever® service, the hotel's 24-hour concierge will provide whatever you want (from a pair of running shoes to private jet service) whenever you need it. Also be sure to take advantage of the just launched 'Wooster Service' that brings an unprecedented level of personal attention to its clients.

For booking enquiries contact Quintessentially Travel
Email: reserve@quintessentiallytravel.com, Tel: +44 (0)845 224 6915

SHANGRI-LA BARR AL JISSAH RESORT & SPA

SULTANATE OF OMAN. COORDINATES – N 23° 33.137, E 58° 39.609

Shangri-La's Barr Al Jissah Resort & Spa sits in a striking bay overlooking the Gulf of Oman, and is backed by rugged mountains. The resort, which comprises three hotels, occupies a vast 124-acre site. Yet you are only 45 minutes from Muscat International Airport and 15 minutes from the city's downtown area. Three hotels make up the complex, which includes the scene-stealing Al Husn (the Castle). This is dramatically set along the cliffs with 170 suites and deluxe guestrooms, all with private balconies and views of the crystal blue waters. Al Husn guests (you have to be over 12 to stay here) benefit from a discreet, personalised butler service, a private gym, reading room, as well as daily complimentary breakfast, afternoon tea and pre-dinner cocktails. There is a 100m-long, residents-only beach and a stunning infinity-edge pool.

Q INSIDER: This is the sort of destination resort you will struggle to leave. Facilities include seven freshwater pools (two interconnected by a current-controlled 'lazy river'), four tennis courts, the Al Mazaar souk, Adventure Zone, marina and dive centre. There are also some 18 bars and restaurants and CHI, The Spa (a Shangri-La signature).

THE CHEDI MUSCAT

MUSCAT, SULTANATE OF OMAN. COORDINATES – N 23° 36.159, E 058° 23.910

The Chedi Muscat opened in January 2003 as an exclusive beach resort in one of the world's most exciting new travel destinations – the Sultanate of Oman on the Indian Ocean. Located on the Boushar Beachfront where crystal clear blue waters reflect Oman's mountain ranges, this modern oasis of Middle Eastern style and contemporary luxury has become one of the most popular resorts in this region for a hit of reliable sun. It's easy to get to, located just 20 minutes from the capital. There's a 370m private beach and three swimming pools – super-chic zones for sleeping under the shade after a morning of body rituals at The Spa. Whether you are here with children or it's just the two of you, The Chedi has flexibility built into its DNA. So whether it's a babysitter you want or a candlelit dinner for two under the stars on the resort's private beach, you can expect your requests to be met with the grace of a resort that prides itself on accurate service and a perfect finish.

Q INSIDER: Chedi Club Suites and Chedi Deluxe Club Rooms have the use of an exclusive retreat called The Library – a private lounge offering complimentary Continental breakfast, morning and afternoon tea, evening cocktails, canapés and free Internet access.

For booking enquiries contact Quintessentially Travel
Email: reserve@quintessentiallytravel.com, Tel: +44 (0)845 224 6915

The eighteenth-century Devi Garh Palace near Udaipur, Rajasthan, took years of restoration to become the all-suite luxury hotel it is today. With a look of modern India, local marbles and semiprecious stones are used to striking effect, offset by the heritage bones of this extraordinary palace in the midst of the Aravali Hills. History abounds, with Devi Garh's village, Delwara, well known for its fourteenth-century Jain temples. All the hotel's 39 suites are unique. The Devi Garh Restaurant offers fine Asian and continental cuisines. Guests can also enjoy evenings at Devi Garh Bar with its eclectic selection of rare whiskeys and wines, accompanied by an array of mouthwatering snacks. There is the option of private dining at special venues, in the numerous lounges, terraces and gardens; you can also practice Yoga and meditation on the ramparts of the palace with the silence broken only by the sounds of running water in the courtyards.

Q INSIDER: This majestic Fort Palace is a perfect place to optimise your wellbeing. There is a gym, steam, sauna and Jacuzzi while The Devi Spa by L'Occitane offers a unique fusion of Mediterranean and Indian wellbeing concepts.

For booking enquiries contact Quintessentially Travel
Email: reserve@quintessentiallytravel.com, Tel: +44 (0)845 224 6915

MIDDLE EAST, ASIA & PACIFIC

Devi Ratn in Jaipur, the new hotel from Devi Resorts, is a 63-suite haven in the heart of the Pink City. Combining lyrical spaces with bold architecture, domes and arches rise out on the horizon while towering structures in red sandstone filter the light of the sun to create patterns on the flooring. All the suites at Devi Ratn are located on crescent-shaped streets at varying heights, ensuring a view of the Aravali mountains from every room. Vibrant gemstone hues and unique black-and-white terrazzo flooring distinguish the spaces. Other interiors reflect Jaipur's gemstone culture with necklace-inspired headboards, study tables and lighting pelmets. Iconic patterns from the nearby Amber Fort are transposed on the glass façade of the poolside restaurant, the etched surfaces reflecting the blue water of the pool. Devi Spa by L'Occitane is one of the largest spas in Asia to be created by this legendary French beauty brand, the 20,000sq ft expanse of white and blue with the gentle sound of water providing perfect counterpoint to the city's rickshaw-packed thoroughfares.

Q INSIDER: Devi Ratn's Luxury Suites are 700 square feet each and open onto a private garden. A necklace of intricate patterns follows you around the room, along the wall and sometimes creating surfaces for seating and furniture.

For booking enquiries contact Quintessentially Travel
Email: reserve@quintessentiallytravel.com, Tel: +44 (0)845 224 6915

RASA JAIPUR

RAJASTHAN, INDIA. COORDINATES – N 27° 00.121, E 075° 52.051

Imagine 40 futuristic tents or cubes rendered in block-printed patterned canvas. These nomadic structures are set against the rocky Nahagarh Hills in a quiet valley towards Jaipur's northern outskirts. One of the hottest hotels to have opened recently in Asia, the project is called Rasa Jaipur – a truly unique Rajasthan experience that is distinctive and authentic yet with the international service and cuisine standards set by the owning family (they also own Devi Garh, the palace-hotel near Udaipur on page 55). Each 500sq ft tent has a high roof that recedes in a slope above the bed. The interiors are done in shades of brown stone, wood and leather giving a sense of pared-down luxury. Textured stone walls offer privacy with all the elements of modern comfort taken care of, including air-conditioning, heating and luxurious bathrooms. When it is time to kick back with a fresh lime soda, guests can enjoy a pavilion extending into a semi-outdoor private space with garden views.

Q INSIDER: Being both of the city and of the country, Rasa Jaipur is very well placed for those who want their hit of Jaipur's extraordinarily good shopping as well as culture at nearby Amber Fort and tiger-spotting adventure at Ranthambore National Park (a two-hour drive away).

THE LEELA PALACE KEMPINSKI UDAIPUR

RAJASTHAN, INDIA. COORDINATES – N 12° 57.658, E 077° 38.936

The Leela Palace Kempinski Udaipur is all about the view for it is perched on the bank of Udaipur's breathtakingly picturesque Lake Pichola. Every single one of the 72 rooms and eight suites overlook this vista, with more besides, including views of the City Palace, Jag Mandir and Lake Palace. Yet not everything about this resort is watery; there are 6.5 acres of gardens and courtyards which, when shared with such relatively few guests, means a panoply of intimate corners for curling up with a book. As is to be expected from this leading brand in Indian five-star hotels, there is a gamut of gourmet riches: The Dining Room serves international cuisine with al fresco dining, The Sheesh Mahal specialises in fine-dining Rajasthan cuisine, while The Library Bar serves single mats to the tunes of Billie Holiday. There is a gym with steam rooms, croquet lawns, even a bocce pitch, with families well catered for.

Q INSIDER: It's hard to know where to begin. A 'heritage view' room overlooking the lake? A city tour in the hotel's custom-designed auto rickshaw? Learning to cook risotto with Kashmir morel mushrooms? Riding across the lake in a custom-made palace boat? Sitting in the rooftop restaurant or lying under the masseur's hands beneath an ESPA tent?

AMANBAGH

RAJASTHAN, INDIA. COORDINATES – N 27° 10.127, E 076° 17.673

The Arravalli Hills in Rajasthan are rugged, myth-rich outcrops sequestering tales dating back to the dawn of Hindu civilisation. Concealed within this vista is Amanbagh in a rural valley 90 minutes from Jaipur. Surrounded by 42 acres of gardens, the resort's wider locale is peppered with hamlets and active markets. This mix of Aman luxury with authentic India is what makes this 40-room resort stand apart, its architecture paying homage to India's Mughal past. A warm welcome is given by all staff who regard you as 'family'; in the villages, locals are equally hospitable, keen to share their culture, from mystical abandoned cities to forgotten temples and forts. At the end of the day Amanbagh's spa offers holistic therapies, yoga, massage and beauty treatments.

Q INSIDER: Safaris in the nearby Sariska Wildlife Reserve offer the opportunity to view tigers, leopards, monkeys and varied birdlife (best from October to February) in their natural habitat. The wider region is open to exploration by horse, jeep and even the occasional elephant.

For booking enquiries contact Quintessentially Travel
Email: reserve@quintessentiallytravel.com, Tel: +44 (0)845 224 6915

ST. REGIS BANGKOK

BANGKOK, THAILAND. COORDINATES – N 13° 44.871, E 100° 32.554

Rajadamri Road is considered Bangkok's key commercial corridor and the choice address of major corporations and elite financial institutions. The St. Regis Bangkok shares this location, and as such, meets the demands of the most discerning kind of traveller. The hotel features a Sky Lounge with panoramic views of the ever-changing landscape of this vibrant city. There is an exclusive Elemis Spa, an inviting outdoor pool, a contemporary poolside cafe, state-of-the-art business centre, superbly appointed function venues and a personable event services team for flawless detials. And Q hasn't even got to the rooms yet... There are 176 of them, ranging from 45 to 250 square metres, as well as 51 suites with floor-to-ceiling windows. While in residence, guests enjoy discreet attention from the signature St. Regis Butlers, whose job it is to attend to every request 24 hours a day.

Q INSIDER: Getting about Bangkok was tricky before the Skytrain. It still is if you've not got a stop on your very doorstep. From the The St. Regis Bangkok, access couldn't be simpler, with the closest station a few minuets walk from the lobby, linking you to all Bangkok's major commercial and business districts.

AMANPURI

PHUKET, THAILAND. COORDINATES – N 07° 59.037, E 098° 16.600

Amanpuri not only put Phuket on the map; it was also the boutique resort that secured Amanresorts' name in Asia and inspired a group of Amanjunkies who have never looked back. Why so? Each of the 40 pavilions is a palace unto itself, located on a dramatic bluff covered with coconut palms. Some 30 private villas (multiple bedrooms, private pools, personal staff) are located on the other side of the plantation. The pool – and this is a feature of most of the group's resorts – makes your heart race; a swatch of green-black tiles flanked by two restaurants. Below lies the Beach Club on a creamy crescent of sand. Aman always gets its locations just right, and Amanpuri is a case in point. Amanpuri has the largest resort-based fleet of cruisers and sailing vessels in South east Asia. Explore the region's limestone outcrops to discover your own private coves and pearly-white beaches.

Q INSIDER: At Amanpuri, you pay for the view. Pavilions 103 and 105 command the best vistas of the Andaman Sea. That said, if you take one of the 25 Superior Garden Pavilions, you won't be short-changed. Concealed by palms, they are totally private.

For booking enquiries contact Quintessentially Travel
Email: reserve@quintessentiallytravel.com, Tel: +44 (0)845 224 6915

TRISARA

PHUKET, THAILAND. COORDINATES – N 08° 02.182, E 098° 16.562

On the Thai island of Phuket, competition is keen among the high-end resorts. Trisara, located on the island's quiet, undeveloped northwest coast, has been a big player in a big game since debut (it was recently voted 'Best Leisure Resort Worldwide' by readers of the influential Gallivanters Guide). The resort is concealed behind ancient hardwood forest just 15 minutes from the island's international airport (direct flights from much of Europe add to Phuket's attractions). Views open up from every villa to embrace soft, natural breezes and a spread of turquoise water framed by two private headlands. It is a sea that more than invites exploration both above and below water. Within the resort, privacy is everything. Forty acres of garden feature just 39 ocean-view pool villas and suites, plus 19 two-to-four bedroom residences each with its own pool. This conspires to make you feel as if the place belongs to you, and only you, with other guest villas concealed by the soft, natural contours of a paradise that has enjoyed the light touch of impeccably good taste from the moment of its inception – that and an obsessive attention to service.

Q INSIDER: This is a family-friendly resort without being swamped by kids. Grown-ups can relax in the spa, do yoga on the beach, or work up a sweat in the gym with a personal trainer. Kids have a club of their own and lots to do with staff arranging outings to nearby islands.

For booking enquiries contact Quintessentially Travel
Email: reserve@quintessentiallytravel.com, Tel: +44 (0)845 224 6915

SRI PANWA ESTATE

PHUKET, THAILAND. COORDINATES – N 7° 48.088, E 98° 24.651

Sri Panwa Estate enjoys an idyllic setting within 40 acres of lush tropical rainforest, on the tip of Thailand's Cape Panwa. With a secluded position 40 to 60 metres above sea level, expect breathtaking views of the Andaman Sea. Of the 51 villas, some boast uninterrupted 300-degrees vistas. Ranging from one to six bedrooms, the standalone houses have been designed in 'tropical contemporary' style, the simple, earthy aesthetic combined with a modern luxury finish. Most recently, the Estate unveiled the Cool Spa and four-storey Baba Poolclub with Cooking School, Hot Pot, Pool Bar, 25m infinity lap pool, business facilities, games room, gym, disco bar and seven new suites. World-class cruising, beach-hopping, snorkeling and scuba diving are literally minutes away from your villa doorstep.

Q INSIDER: The year-round opportunities for boating include visiting eight of the most beautiful islands in the Phuket archipelago. Racha, Maiton, Phi Phi (location of the movie, The Beach), Coral and Lon are all within a 15 to 45 minute journey.

For booking enquiries contact Quintessentially Travel
Email: reserve@quintessentiallytravel.com, Tel: +44 (0)845 224 6915

ANANTARA PHUKET VILLAS

PHUKET. THAILAND. COORDINATES – N 8° 8.696, E 98° 17.863

Anantara Phuket Villas is not only convenient – note the number of direct flights now servicing Phuket – but also delivers a quintessential Thai experience with local textures, tastes and architecture. The property is situated beside serene Mai Khao Beach. The resort's collection of 83 villas, each with a private pool, is framed by Bill Bensley-designed gardens and paths meandering down to the sea. Reminiscent of a southern Thai village, each villa features a spacious living area, Thai furniture and bathroom with an Anantara outdoor 'made for two' terrazzo tub. The feel of the resort is laidback with a large pool flanked by chill-out areas featuring oversized day beds, a bar and soft music. There is also a spa, fully-equipped fitness centre and tennis courts for night play as well as a range of restaurants, from beachside to gourmet.

Q INSIDER: Make the most of Anantara's expertise and join a diving expedition to the Similan Islands. Not that you have to travel far for drama. Nearby the resort are Phang Nga Bay's limestone cliffs poking out above the calm water, with uninhabited sandy strands popular for castaway picnics.

For booking enquiries contact Quintessentially Travel
Email: reserve@quintessentiallytravel.com, Tel: +44 (0)845 224 6915

BAAN TALING NGAM RESORT & SPA

KOH SAMUI, THAILAND. COORDINATES – N 09° 27.189, E 099° 56.213

Koh Samui is one of Thailand's pearls, for it has all the aspects that make for the perfect tropical vacation (including easy access from Bangkok, Hong Kong and Singapore, with numerous daily flights). Baan Taling Ngam Resort & Spa is now among the island's chief draws, built on 22 acres of landscaped grounds in Koh Samui's quiet northeast corner. Guests can choose from over 70 rooms and villas, ranging from eyries perched on cascading hillsides – including 320sq m three-bedroom 'Cliff' residences – to large villas on one of the island's famously white sandy beaches. All are designed in high Thai style with acres of polished teak concealing every conceivable mod-con. Within the grounds you can choose from HOW MANY? fine dining restaurants, a state-of-the-art spa, and a variety of watersports activities as well as mountain biking to explore the island's lush interior and out-of-the-way beaches. We recommend an expedition, if only for a taste of Thai street food during a relaxed, lunchtime sortie.

Q INSIDER: You don't have to extend to the bespoke end of the scale for good service in Thailand. That said, why not have it all? Guests staying in one of Baan Taling Ngam's top residences can reserve an on-call personal 'mae baan', or private housekeeper

W RETREAT KOH SAMUI

KOH SAMUI, THAILAND. COORDINATES – N 09° 34.344, E 100° 01.043

Located between Maenam and Bo Phut, W Retreat Koh Samui can claim one of the most pristine beach locations in southeast Asia, the blue waters of the Gulf of Thailand stretching out in front. The 75 private pool retreats offer all the indulgence and luxury you could possibly wish for: daybeds, an outdoor shower, Yamaha sound system, 47-inch plasma screen TV, wine refrigerator, and the signature W bed. Add to that a treatment at Away Spa, a night of revelry at W Lounge or WooBar – replete with a DJ booth and double-storey wine cellar – and easy dishes at The Kitchen Table or innovative, contemporary Japanese cuisine at Namu. Other diversions include the WET pool, SWEAT state-of-the-art fitness facility, the watersports centre and tennis court. The bustling nightlife of Chaweng is only a mere 10 minutes drive away.

Q INSIDER: W's signature Whatever/Whenever® concierge service provides guests and residents with whatever they want 24/7, from a Champagne brunch on a deserted beach to an impromptu island-hopping excursion.

PANGKOR LAUT RESORT

PERAK, MALAYSIA. COORDINATES – N 04° 11.916, E 100° 32.799

When Pangkor Laut Resort first opened in 1993, it set the benchmark for tropical island luxury the world over. The resort, located on an island only accessible to resort guests, is just a short speedboat ride off Peninsular Malaysia's west coast. Only a fraction of the island's 120 hectares have been developed; the rest is covered by ancient rainforest. Nestled around three secluded bays, the resort blends seamlessly into its jungle island habitat with accommodation designed in the style of a traditional Malay village. These include Sea and Spa Villas standing elegantly over clear emerald waters, Garden and Beach Villas amidst tropical landscaped gardens, and Hill Villas, which include the magnificent Pavarotti Suite, all of which have exceptional views of outlying islands from lofty eyries peaking out from the rainforest canopy. There are seven bars and restaurants with cuisines ranging from local Malaysian delicacies to mouthwatering French dishes.

Q INSIDER: When you tire of the beach (you won't – Emerald Bay is up there in Q's top 10), you can spend time at the resort's award-winning Spa Village. Amidst lotus ponds and herb gardens nestle healing huts and bathhouses offering everything from Chinese herbal to Ayurvedic consultations.

For booking enquiries contact Quintessentially Travel
Email: reserve@quintessentiallytravel.com, Tel: +44 (0)845 224 6915

TANJONG JARA RESORT

TERENGGANU, MALAYSIA. COORDINATES – N 04° 48.692, E 103° 25.399

Inspired by seventeenth-century Malay palaces, Tanjong Jara Resort combines modern, casual chic with warm service and a peerless beachside location on Peninsular Malaysia's east coast. Rooms are a serene collection of elegantly crafted wooden buildings textured with rich fabrics and local hardwood. Bumbung rooms are on the first floor with views of either lush tropical gardens or the South China Sea; the Serambi rooms boast peaceful, shady terraces; Anjung rooms have sunken outdoor baths within private courtyards. Dining at the resort includes authentic Malaysian cuisine at Di Atas Sungei, which sits above the river. Seafood is found at Nelayan and light, poolside lunches at Teratai Terrace. There is an award-winning spa deemed among the world's most innovative by Tatler magazine, as well as amazing opportunities for seasonal diving in nearby Terengganu Marine Park.

Q INSIDER: The Anjung Suite rests on stilts above the river, with a living and dining area, bar and powder room and an extended balcony with striking views of the beach and South China Sea.

For booking enquiries contact Quintessentially Travel
Email: reserve@quintessentiallytravel.com, Tel: +44 (0)845 224 6915

THE CLUB AT THE SAUJANA

SELANGOR, MALAYSIA. COORDINATES – N 03° 06.501, E 101° 34.708

Saujana is a word that originates from an old Malay expression, 'sejauh d sana', which means 'as far as the eye can see'. And at The Club at The Saujana your eyes are in for a veritable visual treat. Situated 30 minutes from the city o Kuala Lumpur and 35 minutes from Kuala Lumpur International Airport (KLIA) The Club at The Saujana is carved out of a 160-acre former palm and rubbe plantation boasting lush tropical gardens set amongst rolling hills and large tranquil lakes. The resort is designed by Jaya Ibrahim of Jaya & Associates, an award-winning Indonesian interior designer; it offers 105 rooms and suites fashioned in an elegant boutique style. The distinctive contemporary Asian style lends itself perfectly to the ambient tones, personalised service and meticulous detail, and tastefully respects important elements of Malaysian culture and architecture. If you're planning the honeymoon trip of a lifetime the one and only Saujana Suite could be your 'dream come true'. A luxurious retreat with breathtaking views of the lake and the golf course, a sumptuous and spacious home away from home with its elegant dining room, living room and state-of-the-art entertainment facilities, not to mention the bedroom with a view that connects to an expansive walk-in wardrobe.

Q Insider: Pamper yourself in the steam sauna or even better – share a romantic spa experience with your loved one in the couple treatment room.

For booking enquiries contact Quintessentially Travel
Email: reserve@quintessentiallytravel.com, Tel: +44 (0)845 224 6915

RAFFLES HOTEL, SINGAPORE

SINGAPORE. COORDINATES – N 01° 17.680, E 103° 51.282

Combining an architectural classic of the colonial era with the sleek service of the Raffles Group, which now manages eight hotels worldwide, Raffles Hotel, Singapore is one of Asia's great heritage addresses. Like The Strand in Yangon, Raffles Hotel, Singapore was founded by the Sarkies brothers in 1887. In 2011 the hotel remains at the top of its form: impeccably maintained gardens of close-cut lawn, excellent cuisine in its restaurants (if you're just in on a flight, slip into the 1920s-style Empire Cafe for a bowl of simple laksa), with breakfast taken on the shaded verandas which stretch between rooms. There are 103 suites, each tastefully appointed with period furnishings and modern conveniences. There is also a pool to escape that tropical heat, and a Raffles Spa. For a true taste of a classic, pop into The Long Bar for a 'Singapore Sling' (this was where the eponymous cocktail was born).

Q INSIDER: If Singapore is a paradise for gourmands and shoppers, you don't have to travel far to experience it. Raffles Hotel, Singapore is a complete world in itself, featuring 15 restaurants and bars while the adjoining Raffles Hotel Arcade houses over 40 international and regional specialty stores.

For booking enquiries contact Quintessentially Travel
Email: reserve@quintessentiallytravel.com, Tel: +44 (0)845 224 6915

THE FULLERTON HOTEL
SINGAPORE

SINGAPORE. COORDINATES – N 01° 17.176, E 103° 51.173

A perfect blend of old wired with the new, this 1928 Palladian-style Singapore landmark was recast in 2001 as a 400-room luxury hotel. The Fullerton Hotel is all about calm, from the soft vanilla-coloured walls to the outdoor infinity pool. Yet you are also at the heart of the action. The hotel is located in the Central Business District, just minutes from the main shopping belt and overlooking the historic Singapore River. Rooms and suites have impressive views. Broadband connectivity provides guests with wired and wireless high-speed Internet access. You have also got a luxury spa, 24-hour gym and numerous dining options, including Italian, Japanese, Asian and modern Chinese cuisines, and the stylish Post Bar. And all so discreet, right down to the way polished shoes are dispatched through a specially designed niche in your wardrobe.

Q INSIDER: Ask for a suite with a panoramic view of the Singapore River or sea. Coupled with The Fullerton's approach to quiet, understated service, an all-encompassing sense of calm will still even the most frenetic mind.

THE FULLERTON BAY HOTEL

SINGAPORE. COORDINATES – N 01° 16.999, E 103° 51.185

The Fullerton Bay Hotel opened summer 2010 with 100 rooms and suites – all with floor-to-ceiling windows offering views of the hotel's prime waterfront location on Singapore's Marina Bay. The hotel is ensconced between Clifford Pier and Customs House – both iconic historic buildings. The bustling dining and entertainment hubs Boat Quay and Clarke Quay, are nearby, as well as cultural centres including Chinatown, the Victoria Theatre, Concert Hall and Singapore Art Museum. Orchard Road's shopping is nearby. Not that you want to wander far. The Fullerton Bay Hotel features breathtaking architecture and glamorous interiors by highly acclaimed Asian designers: an expansive 17m-wide lobby by Andre Fu who has also done the hotel's three restaurants – Lantern, Clifford and The Landing Point.

Q INSIDER: Guests enjoy access to a round-the-clock gym located on the rooftop. There is also a 25m infinity pool on this lofty perch – a truly striking scene-stealer in a city that right now is reaching for the sky with numerous multi-million dollar developments.

For booking enquiries contact Quintessentially Travel
Email: reserve@quintessentiallytravel.com, Tel: +44 (0)843 224 6915

AMANKILA

BALI, INDONESIA. COORDINATES – S 8° 33.011, E 115° 28.835

What makes Amankila stand apart from Bali's formidable competition is its pulse-quickening location on a dramatic cliff and beach overlooking the Lombok Strait on the island's east coast. All 34 freestanding suites make the most of this eyrie while the architecture speaks of Amankila's connection to the local heritage. The resort is in Karangasem, Bali's most traditional regency. So the suites, like palaces, reflect royal design motifs (you will see the connection when you stop by Ujung, the water palace outside Amlapura). The showstopper is the resort's main pool – three infinity tiers in rich green tiles to reflect the colour of the ocean. There is a Beach Club at the base of the cliff, and another large pool in a coconut grove. The three restaurants serve Indonesian and Western cuisine.

Q INSIDER: The pool suites are a must (there are nine, and be warned, they always sell first). Q's recommendations have to include The Indrakila Suite, Kilasari Suite (this one with a 12m pool), and the two-bedroom Amankila Suite with a spirit-lifting, sea-facing terrace.

For booking enquiries contact Quintessentially Travel
Email: reserve@quintessentiallytravel.com, Tel: +44 (0)845 224 6915

AYANA
RESORT & SPA BALI

BALI, INDONESIA. COORDINATES – S 08° 47.172, E 115° 08.320

Voted 'Number One Spa Hotel in the World' at the 2010 Condé Nast Traveller Readers' Awards, and most recently 'Asia's Leading Luxury Villa and Luxury Resort 'at the World Travel Awards 2010, AYANA Resort and Spa Bali is a hard act to beat. Not least the location, the resort perched on limestone cliffs above the Indian Ocean near Jimbaran Bay on Bali's southwest peninsula. Featuring 78 freestanding luxury villas and a 290-room hotel, the 77-hectare property enjoys majestic views across its 1.3 kilometre coastline – this includes a secluded white-sand beach – yet is an accessible 15-minute ride from the airport. Highlights include the Thermes Marins Bali Spa with one of the world's largest Aquatonic Pools and the spectacular 'Spa on the Rocks' treatment villas. There are freshwater swimming pools as well as one salt-water, infinity-edged Ocean Beach Pool, an 18-hole golf putting course and some 13 dining venues.

Q INSIDER: The new Rock Bar is built on natural rock 14 metres above the ocean at the base of towering cliffs. For a dramatic sundowner, only Tanah Lot on the island's southernmost tip beats this for location. Or maybe AYANA's three-bedroom presidential villa with its 11m-long infinity pool.

For booking enquiries contact Quintessentially Travel
Email: reserve@quintessentiallytravel.com, Tel: +44 (0)845 224 6915

CHINA WORLD SUMMIT WING

BEIJING, CHINA. COORDINATES – N 39° 54.821, E 116° 27.502

In a city of extremes, China World Summit Wing, Beijing, is the tallest hotel in the capital. It occupies the upper floors of Beijing's newest iconic landmark, the 330m-tall China World Tower, and as such, forms part of the integrated China World Trade Center complex with direct links to the city's coveted designer shopping opportunities in the China World Mall. Close to the historic centre, this central business district location has it all – whatever your reasons for being in Beijing, whether for a high-profile conference or to tool about The Forbidden City. There are 278 guestrooms and suites (the average room size is a generous 65 square metres), four restaurants, a bar, lounge and four private dining venues (the most coveted is an observation deck on level 81). CHI, the city's highest spa retreat, is on level 77 with a 25m indoor infinity pool overlooking the urban hubbub.

Q INSIDER: With service hallmarks such as a personal shopper on demand and floor butlers, China World Summit Wing, Beijing, ensures English-speaking guests are made to feel entirely at ease in a city that can sometimes seem inscrutable.

For booking enquiries contact Quintessentially Travel
Email: reserve@quintessentiallytravel.com, Tel: +44 (0)845 224 6915

AMAN AT SUMMER PALACE

BEIJING, CHINA. COORDINATES – N 39° 59.914, E 116° 16.300

Beijing's Summer Palace is among Asia's most important cultural jewels, built in 1750 as the favoured abode of the Empress Dowager Cixi. Cut to 2011 and just steps from its East Gate lies Aman at Summer Palace, Beijing, housed in a series of dwellings, some of which once served as guest quarters for those awaiting an audience with the Empress. They have been enriched with the artful Aman eye, the 44 rooms and suites featuring screens, bamboo blinds, four-poster beds and Ming dynasty-inspired furniture. The tranquil atmosphere is the kind you can imagine fit for princesses gliding, with barely a rustle of silk, between secret assignations. There is a Chinese restaurant, three other restaurants including The Grill and Naoki, a bar, cigar room, fitness centre, 25m indoor lap pool, spa, library and boutique.

Q INSIDER: Be sure to give the city at least three nights. Aman guides will be able to offer guests a glimpse of Beijing many visitors miss out on, from secret boutiques, restaurants, bars and art galleries to the atmospheric hutongs and 'old' neighbourhoods.

H■MA CHATEAU

GUILIN, CHINA. COORDINATES – N 25° 03.030, E 110° 20.026

HOMA – Hotel of Modern Art is often cited as the mother of the design hotel phenomenon in mainland China – an extraordinary 46-room bolthole by Tracy Wen inside Yuzi Paradise, a stunning 550-hectare art park filled with some 150 contemporary monumental sculptures amid Guilin's limestone peaks (the famous 'karst' formations of the postcards). The brainchild of Rhy Chang Tsao, a Taiwanese billionaire, this Relais & Chateaux property not only looks unique – grass-covered rooftops, experimental architectural forms – but also delivers on the detail. There are two restaurants, including Lotus for Western and Asian fusion cuisine. Service smoothes the way for Western guests: from the moment you arrive at the airport you are paired with a trained Host – a sort of personal concierge – for the duration of your stay.

Q INSIDER: While most people will be satisfied with just walking the park and experiencing the sculpture, be sure to leave enough time to explore the local area with a visit to the rice terraces in Longsheng, and bamboo rafting on the Yulong River.

For booking enquiries contact Quintessentially Travel
Email: reserve@quintessentiallytravel.com, Tel: +44 (0)845 224 6915

TH▮ PENINSULA H▮NG KONG

HONG KONG, CHINA
COORDINATES – N 22° 17.693, E 114° 10.308

When it opened in 1928, The Peninsula Hong Kong was quick to win the title 'Grande Dame of the Far East'. It has a stellar location on Victoria Harbour in the heart of Kowloon's shopping, business and entertainment district. You can take The Peninsula's service as a given. Then there are the hard facts. The hotel's 300 rooms and suites combine a quiet, nostalgic aesthetic with advanced technological innovations. There's a fitness centre and a huge Roman-style swimming pool that opens onto the hotel's Sun Terrace to provide sweeping views of Victoria Harbour and Hong Kong Island. The Peninsula Spa by ESPA is a 14-room oasis. In terms of restaurants, Gaddi's is one of the leading French restaurants in Asia, while Felix is a stylish, Philippe Starck-designed rendezvous. Afternoon Tea at The Lobby is a Hong Kong institution, and some of the best authentic Cantonese food in town is served in Spring Moon.

Q INSIDER: The 14 Rolls-Royce Phantoms, together with The Peninsula's helicopter shuttle service from the hotel's rooftop helipad (the only one in Hong Kong), offer guests easy access to the airport as well as aerial tours around the city. Newly-launched MINI Coopers are complimentary to all suite guests for three hours daily.

For booking enquiries contact Quintessentially Travel
Email: reserve@quintessentiallytravel.com, Tel: +44 (0)845 224 6915

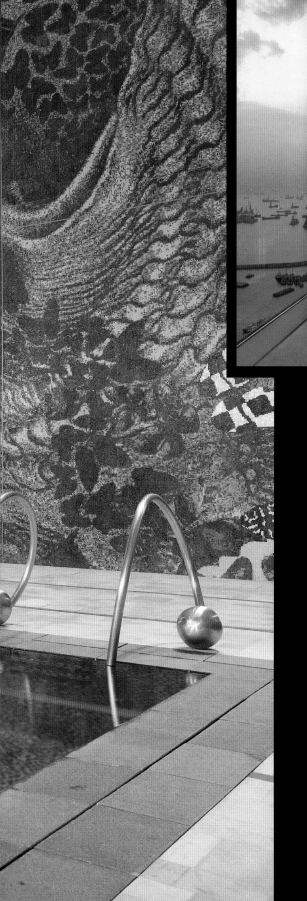

W HONG KONG

HONG KONG, CHINA. COORDINATES – N 22° 18.316, E 114° 09.660

W Hong Kong likes to say it puts the 'chi' in chic with the natural elements of wood, fire, earth, metal and water woven throughout the hotel's architecture. Located beside the Victoria Harbour in the electric new district of West Kowloon, W Hong Kong is young, fashionable and vibrant. This spirit is perfectly embodied in the hotel's main lounge, Living Room, where creative dim sum is served by day and where DJs and mixologists perform against Hong Kong's dramatic skyline by night. Guest rooms take the hotel's 'Whatever/Whenever' attitude to another plateau. The giveaway is in the names: Wonderful, Spectacular, Fabulous and Cool Corner, with suites defined as Fantastic, Marvelous, WOW and EXTREME WOW. Restaurants include Kitchen for pan-Asian and international specialties served up in casual surroundings, and Fire, which makes artful use of the grill. To enjoy all this – as well as fast-track access to the city's hottest nightspots – book one of W Hong Kong's Audi Q7 limos for your pick-up from Chek Lap Kok airport.

Q INSIDER: W Hong Kong is home to Asia's first Bliss® spa as well as the city's highest swimming pool located a whopping 211 metres above ground (keep an ear out for the seasonal pool parties where the great and good can be found dancing among the stars). An aside to shoppers: the hotel is located next to the city's newest luxury mall.

ISLAND SHANGRI-LA

HONG KONG, CHINA. COORDINATES – N 22° 16.606, E 114° 09.866

If a city hotel is all about location, then Island Shangri-La in Hong Kong comes up trumps. It bursts out of the heart of the city's Central district, rising directly from Pacific Place, which Hong Kongers will tell you is among the most prestigious shopping and entertainment complexes. On an island famously pinched for space, Island Shangri – La prides itself on the fact the 565 luxury rooms and suites are among the largest in Hong Kong; all of them have views of either the Peak or Victoria Harbour. Interiors combine Asian – accented European furnishings – a transcontinental mix carried through to the gourmet offerings. Among the restaurants, there is the Michelin – starred Restaurant Petrus for gastronomic French, as well as Nadaman for traditional Japanese kaiseki. The Health Club includes an outdoor swimming pool (heated in the winter), indoor and outdoor Jacuzzis, a steam and sauna.

Q INSIDER: Those reaching for the heights should book a Horizon Club room on the hotel's upper floors. Extra privileges include access to the highest executive lounge in the city for evening cocktails, continental breakfast, a private check – in and use of a private meeting room.

For booking enquiries contact Quintessentially Travel
Email: reserve@quintessentiallytravel.com, Tel: +44 (0)845 224 6915

FUCHUN RESORT

HANGZHOU, CHINA. COORDINATES – N 30° 04.786, E 120° 02.173

While most city dwellers tend to escape to the shore, Shanghai natives head inland to Fuchun Resort. The property is set within 148 hectares of hillside tea plantation in the lake district of Fuyang near Hangzhou – a location inspired by the 700-year-old 'Dwelling in the Fuchun Mountain' by Huang Gong-Wang (the Yuan dynasty's greatest painter). The resort's serene spirit can be felt throughout the rooms and suites with the top five hillside villas set atop lush, green, tea-planted hills. Each villa, designed by Jean-Michel Gathy, features the Fuchun signature: a dramatic private indoor swimming pavilion. The resort's spa offers sessions of Himalayan yoga whereas active travellers will gravitate towards the 18-hole Golf Club, a Par-72 course sculpted from the tea-covered hills by Gary Player's chief designer, Daniel J. Obermyer. Key experiences include dinner at Club-8 – one of the resort's three restaurants – and sipping Mingqian Longjing tea in the Lake Lounge at sunset.

Q INSIDER: The resort is well connected with Hangzhou train station a mere 30-minute drive away and in under an hour Hangzhou International Airport offers numerous direct flights from all over Asia including Singapore, Japan, Malaysia and Taiwan.

For booking enquiries contact Quintessentially Travel
Email: reserve@quintessentiallytravel.com, Tel: +44 (0)845 224 6915

PARK HYATT TOKYO

TOKYO, JAPAN. COORDINATES – N 35° 41.115, E 139° 41.443

High in the sky above Japan's busiest city is Park Hyatt Tokyo. With its dramatic perch on the top 14 floors of the 52-storey Shinjuku Park Tower, the hotel affords sweeping views of the city. Designed primarily as a private urban residence, the hotel's 177 guestrooms (including 23 suites) feature a distinguishing modern interior design and private art collection. The New York Grill & Bar is a landmark venue on the 52nd floor with 360-degree views of Tokyo (you will recognise it from Sophia Ford Coppola's movie, 'Lost in Translation'). Best of all, if you're a non-Japanese speaker in this famously inscrutable country, then you can count on the concierge desk to unravel any local logistics or complex communications (they will also help you obtain local cell phones – a Tokyo necessity).

Q INSIDER: The Tokyo Suite, situated on the 50th floor, has views of the city stretching to Mount Fiji. The 220sq m modernist private residence has been created by Hong Kong-based designer, John Morford. Bibliophiles will love the suite's 1,000-book strong private library.

For booking enquiries contact Quintessentially Travel
Email: reserve@quintessentiallytravel.com, Tel: +44 (0)845 224 6915

THE LODGE AT TARRALEAH

TASMANIA, AUSTRALIA. COORDINATES – S 42° 18.058, E 146° 27.011

To be in Tasmania and make the Condé Nast Traveller 'Hot List' is no mean achievement. But then, if you are this far into the wilds, you might as well go the full distance. The Lodge at Tarreleah is a remarkable, nine-suite lodge a 90-minute drive from Hobart occupying a 300-acre site on a plateau overlooking UNESCO World Heritage wilderness crisscrossed with lakes, rivers and streams. The detail is immaculate from mohair throws to bespoke Tasmanian art in every room, oversized marble bathrooms and a cliff-top spa. You can enjoy adventure by day – golf to a chorus of kookaburras, fishing, breakfast with a platypus – and indulgence by night, with exceptional cuisine showcasing Tasmania's seasonal produce. The property is open year-round, and is ideal for a group of friends seeking to take over a house in its entirety.

Q INSIDER: Ask for a meeting with Hans Naarding – the last man to have seen a Tasmanian tiger alive and the head wildlife guide for the hotel.

WOLGAN VALLEY RESORT & SPA

NEW SOUTH WALES, AUSTRALIA. COORDINATES – S 33° 15.245, E 150° 11.011

Wolgan Valley Resort & Spa offers the rare opportunity to experience a spectacular Australian landmark location. Billing itself as the country's first luxury conservation-based resort, Wolgan is a three-hour drive from Sydney and borders the Greater Blue Mountains World Heritage Area. Ergo: you are nestled between two National Parks, your exact location within 4,000 private acres at the foot of towering cliffs. There are 40 individual suites, each with its own deck and swimming pool. The main 1832 Homestead offers distinctive dining, luxury facilities and a stand-alone spa with six double treatment rooms. With architecture reminiscent of traditional rural Australian homesteads, the experience is anything but rough and ready. Instead it is a place to experience an extraordinary natural sanctuary, witness wildlife and wilderness and rediscover that sense of true relaxation.

Q INSIDER: Don't stay for less than four nights. There are numerous nature-based activities including four-wheel-drive safaris, guided nature walks, mountain bike excursions, heritage interpretive tours, nature walks and horse riding.

HUKA LODGE

CENTRAL PLATEAU, NEW ZEALAND
COORDINATES – S 38° 39.268, E 176° 05.159

You can't talk about New Zealand without mentioning Huka Lodge – one of the country's most iconic retreats. Since the 1920s, it has been a best-kept secret amongst the world's most discerning travellers. This is where royalty, heads of state, business leaders, actors and authors often seek rest and relaxation from everyday life beside the hypnotic turquoise waters of the Waikato River, within 17 acres of peace and beauty. The 18 Lodge Rooms, one suite and two cottages are nestled on a riverbank within a protected nature reserve in a part of the country renowned for its crisp, clean air. There are forests, snow-capped mountains, rivers, streams and the magnificence of Lake Taupo all nearby. Guests can enjoy golf, horseriding, river rafting, trout fishing, nature walks and mountain biking. They can also expect seamless service and gourmet cuisine – with over 20 sublime, and deliberately romantic, private dining venues to choose from.

Q INSIDER: If you're travelling with extended family or friends, consider The Owner's Cottage and its newly-opened companion, the Alan Pye Cottage, featuring four and two suites respectively. Both have a personal butler and chef as well as large outdoor decks and infinity pools.

For booking enquiries contact Quintessentially Travel
Email: reserve@quintessentiallytravel.com, Tel: +44 (0)845 224 6915

EAGLES NEST

NEW ZEALAND. COORDINATES – S 35° 15.162, E 174° 6.991

Eagles Nest is an award-winning retreat set atop its own 75-acre private peninsula overlooking New Zealand's spectacular Bay of Islands. Designed and furnished in an eclectic international contemporary style, it is made up of five villas, sleeping from two to eight, each with its own private heated horizon-edged lap pool, Jacuzzi, air conditioning, wireless Internet access, original artworks, home theatre system and fully equipped gourmet kitchen. The team of talented resident personal chefs offer menus featuring freshly caught fish, venison, lamb, crayfish and more. In addition, you can make use of the estate's personal trainer, spa therapists and concierge services to organise worldclass big game fishing, scenic cruising, sailing, diving, kayaking, bush walking, mountain biking, helicopter flights and romantic picnics on any one of the 150 dots that make up this extraordinary wilderness. Put another way, Eagles Nest has got it all.

Q INSIDER: The Rahimoana Villa comes with its own Porsche Cayenne Turbo for guests to use locally. Not that you have to drive far. The pretty township of Russell – with its cafés, restaurants and quaint seaside charm – is within walking distance of the estate.

For booking enquiries contact Quintessentially Travel
Email: reserve@quintessentiallytravel.com, Tel: +44 (0)843 224 6915

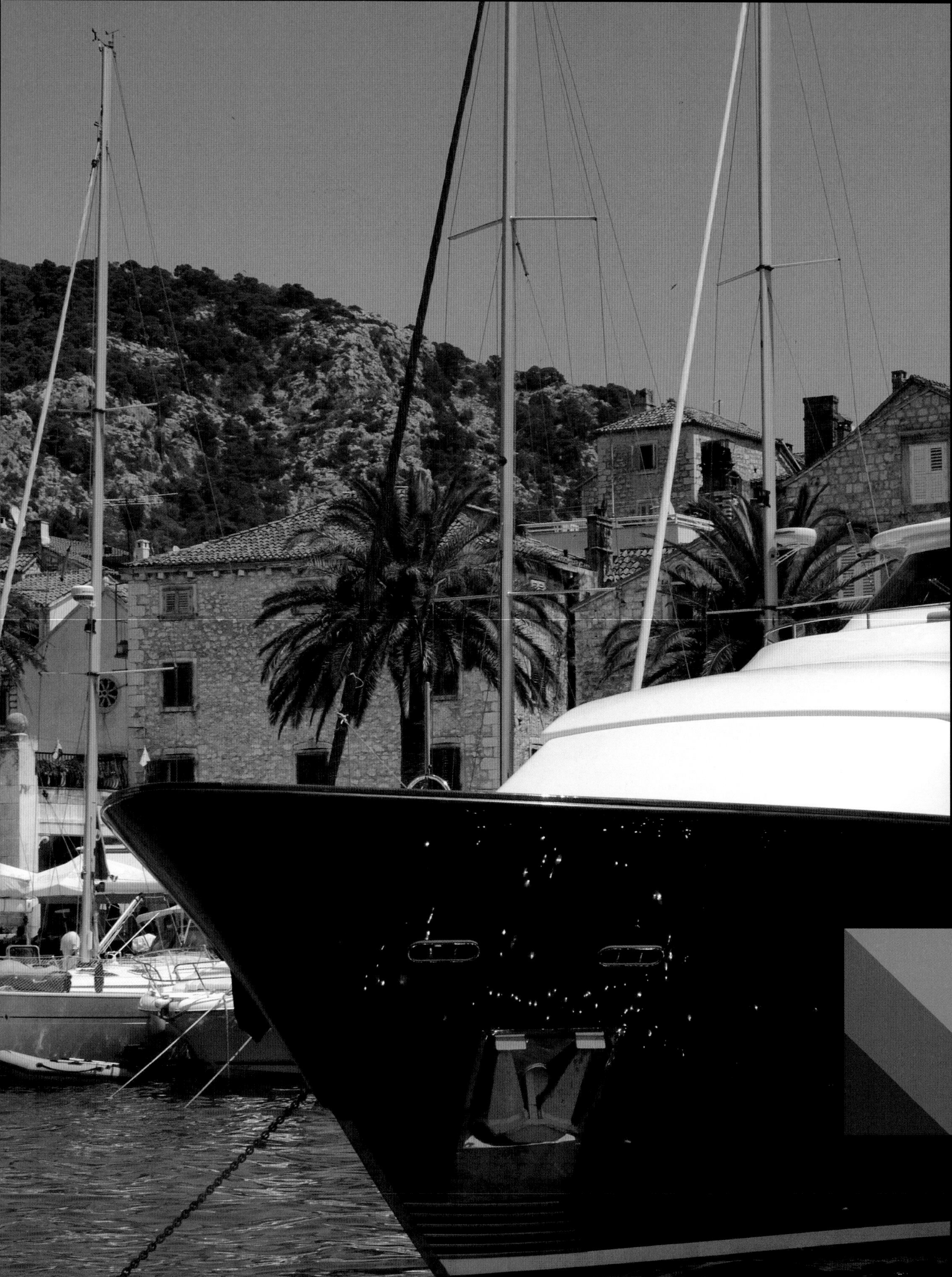

EUROPE

HOTEL D'ANGLETERRE

COPENHAGEN, DENMARK. COORDINATES – N 55° 40.834, E 012° 35.070

Hotel D´Angleterre is all about classic luxury within a unique historic setting in the heart of Copenhagen. The 123-room, 255-year-old hotel overlooks Kings Square, which is about the best address you could hope for. With such an impressive location you have ample opportunity to experience this prettiest of cities; within easy walking distance you will find the Royal Danish Theatre, The Royal Palace, House of Parliament and Strøget, which is the world's longest pedestrian shopping street. Kongens Nytorv Metro Station is a 50m wander from the hotel lobby (this is the heart of the hotel, and abuzz with guests passing through Copenhagen, winter and summer). Modern technology and individually designed suites conspire to make you feel entirely at ease, while the hotel's eponymous Michelin-recommended restaurant can claim to be a gourmet destination in its own right.

Q INSIDER: The spa at Hotel D´Angleterre features Scandinavia's largest indoor hotel pool. Together with the steam bath, sauna and Jacuzzi, this refuge makes for a welcome salve after all that walking about town.

For booking enquiries contact Quintessentially Travel
Email: reserve@quintessentiallytravel.com, Tel: +44 (0)845 224 6915

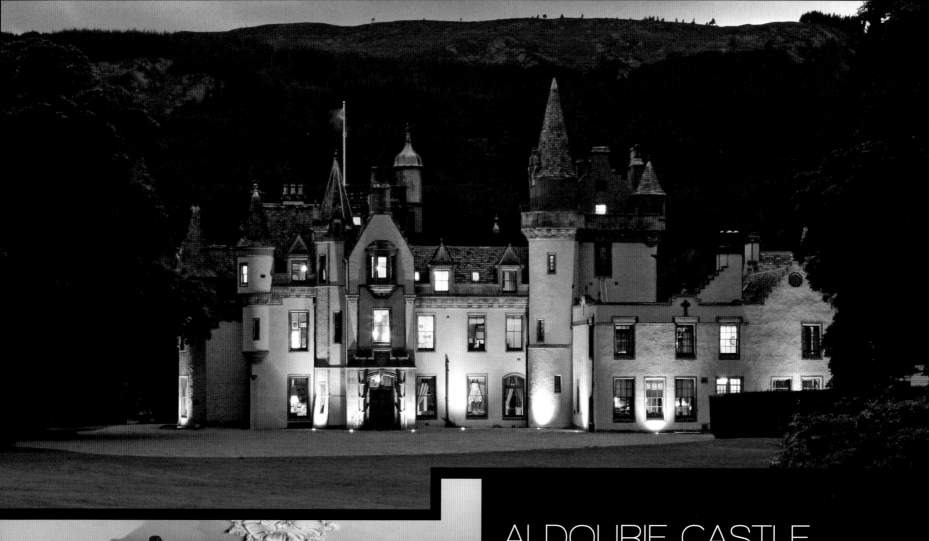

ALDOURIE CASTLE ESTATE

INVERNESS, SCOTLAND. COORDINATES – N 57° 24.223, W 004° 19.778

Aldourie Castle Estate is an exclusive-use property available to hire for a day, week or longer. Located at the head of Loch Ness, a more dramatic Highland positioning is hard to imagine. Carrying the Grade A listing for its jostling, fairytale turrets and towers, this is a Scottish pile that might date back to 1626 but in 2011 feels the warming hand of impeccable staff and first-class cuisine as well as painstakingly restored interiors. The 15-room castle sleeps a maximum of 28 guests who get the run of some 500 acres of forests and woodland on the loch's southern shore. Everyone has room to relax, while a series of spiral staircases and one elevator leads to guestrooms replete with four-poster beds. From your windows the big outdoors is forever beckoning with fishing, hiking, cycling and trips out on the water, as well as golf at Dornoch and even a little 'Nessie' hunting.

Q INSIDER: With its easy, accessible location just a 30-minute drive from Inverness Airport, you can leave London at teatime and be in the Highlands in time for a pre-dinner whisky.

For booking enquiries contact Quintessentially Travel.
Email: reserve@quintessentiallytravel.com, Tel: +44 (0)845 224 6915

ALLADALE WILDERNESS LODGE & RESERVE

SUTHERLAND, SCOTLAND. COORDINATES – N 57° 52.173, W 004° 38.001

Alladale Wilderness Lodge & Reserve is a place to put down the BlackBerry and hunker down in cosy solitude with family or friends. Or to walk, bike, fly-fish, horseride or play golf (there are six courses within an hour's drive including the world-famous Royal Dornoch). An exclusive-use property, Alladale lies deep in the Scottish Highlands; from the highest point on the reserve you can see both the North Sea and Atlantic Ocean. The property is made up of three stone lodges that can be hired together or separately. The main lodge sleeps up to 14 guests; stay here and you benefit from a full-board service with Alladale's resident chef. Guests also have use of snooker room, TV room, sauna, gym and treatment room. Eagles Crag, completed in 2009, is best suited to four adults and four children while Ghillie's Rest is the more intimate option, ideal for a couple and two kids.

Q INSIDER: Both the smaller houses operate a 'crofters kitchen service' whereby fridges are well stocked for self-service breakfasts and lunches; suppers consist of hearty meals prepared by the lodge kitchen and delivered daily for simple re-heating.

For booking enquiries contact Quintessentially Travel
Email: reserve@quintessentiallytravel.com, Tel: +44 (0)845 224 6915

LISMORE CASTLE

LISMORE, IRELAND
COORDINATES – N 52° 08.396, W 007° 55.966

Lismore Castle sits at the heart of a one of the most beautiful, historic privately owned estates in Ireland – and is available for exclusive rent throughout the year. Located in the southern county of West Waterford, this is the perfect choice for a super-exclusive house party, the castle consisting of 15 bedrooms and 14 bathrooms. Unlike so many Irish properties of this size, the property is dearly loved, with every comfort accounted for; understated elegance and old-fashioned luxury therefore emanate from every pore. A personal butler and his team look after guests, offering a unique level of personal attention, luxury and service. The ground floor has a drawing room, two sitting rooms, dining room (seats up to 24), hall and Banqueting Hall (seats up to 80). Fine food is the highlight of any guest's stay, with chefs using locally sourced and home produced ingredients, everything made from scratch in the Castle kitchens.

Q INSIDER: Lismore Castle boasts a superb concierge service to help guests plan and arrange every aspect of their trip from helicopter transfers, to private yoga classes as well as tennis, fishing, golf, guided tours of the lovingly maintained private gardens and Lismore's world-class art collection.

For booking enquiries contact Quintessentially Travel
Email: reserve@quintessentiallytravel.com, Tel: +44 (0)845 224 6915

THE GROVE

HERTFORDSHIRE, ENGLAND
COORDINATES – N 51° 40.643, W 000° 26.188

Everything about The Grove, a lovingly restored Grade II-listed mansion, works with the smooth and friendly efficiency of a hotel with experience. The crisp, sleek, interiors co-exist comfortably with the historical legacy and 21st-century technology. The location is both of the city and the country, located 30 minutes from both Heathrow and Central London. Yet The Grove has views of the bucolic Hertfordshire countryside (the Grand Union canal meanders through the grounds). Bedrooms and suites range from the luxurious to the truly palatial. The West Wing rooms are the ultimate in contemporary style and comfort and the uniquely designed Mansion rooms, many with fireplaces and four-poster beds, are beyond lavish. Facilities include an 18-hole championship golf course, which hosted the 2006 World Golf Championships, three restaurants and bars (including Colette's for gastronomic modern British cuisine), Anouska's Kids' Club, 23 meeting rooms and a Walled Garden complete with an outdoor heated pool, tennis courts and a luxury 'beach' in the summer.

Q INSIDER: Sequoia Spa at The Grove is among the leading destination spas in England, with a full gamut of facilities that includes a 22m indoor pool, 12 individual treatment rooms and one double suite. Therapists use ESPA products with a special focus on Ayurvedic treatments.

For booking enquiries contact Quintessentially Travel
Email: reserve@quintessentiallytravel.com, Tel: +44 (0)845 224 6915

HOTEL ENDSLEIGH

DEVON, ENGLAND. COORDINATES – N 50° 34.848, W 004° 16.034

Olga Polizzi is the style maven who redefined British seaside chic with Hotel Tresanton in St Mawes, Cornwall. Hotel Endsleigh is another of her projects, located on the fringe of Dartmoor in rural Devon. The grand Regency home is positioned in a thickly wooded dell above the River Tamar 10 minutes drive from Tavistock. Wander freely among 108 acres of Humphry Repton-designed gardens, including bamboo-shaded streams, grottoes and rhododendrons. Much of the original interior has been retained, including panelling in the drawing rooms, stained glass windows and gorgeous hand-painted period wallpapers. There are 16 rooms with soft chintzes, antique-fitted bathrooms, and throughout, that inimitable subtle Polizzi soul. This relaxed sensibility, combined with Endsleigh's modern English cuisine, makes you wish you had stayed for more than a weekend.

Q INSIDER: No two rooms are the same, allowing you to keep coming back for a fresh experience. With that in mind, a Q favourite is Room 8 with hand-painted wallpaper and French windows that frame the River Tamar. Room 5 is another beauty, this one with Chinese wallpaper.

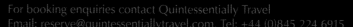

For booking enquiries contact Quintessentially Travel
Email: reserve@quintessentiallytravel.com, Tel: +44 (0)845 224 6915

THE DORCHESTER

LONDON, ENGLAND. COORDINATES – N 51° 30.427, W 000° 09.140

London and The Dorchester are simply indivisible. The hotel opened in 1931 with a Park Lane location consisting of 250 rooms and suites decorated in a classic English residential style. Prince Philip hosted his stag night in the hotel's Park Suite—and the glamour keeps coming, from Hollywood A-listers to the rock fraternity. What is conspicuous is this hotel is continually receiving some of the best investment in the industry. The Krug Room and The Dorchester Spa were remodelled just recently. The Bar at The Dorchester is one of London's hottest meeting spots, and the British Tea Council keeps naming The Dorchester's afternoon tea as the capital's best. Everything is on your doorstep: the West End's theatres, Mayfair's clubs and Sloane Street's shops. A tip: book the remodelled rooftop suites for contemporary interiors and Hyde Park views. And even if you're not staying, at least have dinner at the hotel's contemporary French Alain Ducasse restaurant- the only UK hotel restaurant to hold three Michelin stars.

Q INSIDER: The Dorchester Spa is where to find renowned facialist Vaishaly, new discovery Carol Joy London, and Kerstin Florian. The spa features nine treatment rooms, including two double suites, and even a 'Spatisserie' for sweet treats.

CLARIDGE'S

LONDON, ENGLAND. COORDINATES – N 51° 30.739, W 0° 8.848

Glamorous, elegant and alive with laughter, Claridge's is for true connoisseurs of luxury at a time when the real deal counts more than anything. A century of hustle, bustle and style contributes to the hotel's uniquely sophisticated ambience in the heart of Mayfair. Yet the feeling is still young, fresh and dynamic, attracting those fashion designers on the tip of everyone's tongue as well as the old guard who can't give up their Claridge's addiction (the ladies' powder room does it for one and all, says handbag designer Lulu Guinness). There is the elegant Foyer where you can take afternoon tea, cocktails in the hotel's glittering bar, the Art Deco Reading Room for delicious all-day dining, and the legendary cuisine of Gordon Ramsay at Claridge's. The room that bottles the spirit most perfectly of all has to be the sumptuous Thirties-inspired Fumoir – an intimate, velvet-lined room for enjoying the world's finest cognacs, armagnacs, rums, tequilas and ports. Individually crafted by top designers, the hotel's rooms and suites mix the best modern comforts with stunning original pieces to impart that feeling of timeless English glamour.

Q INSIDER: Check out the new rooms and suites created by royal designers Linley and Diane von Furstenberg for the height of luxury.

For booking enquiries contact Quintessentially Travel
Email: reserve@quintessentiallytravel.com, Tel: +44 (0)845 224 6915

THE SAVOY

LONDON, ENGLAND. COORDINATES – N 51° 30.622, W 000° 07.251

A British icon since 1889, The Savoy has recently undergone one of the most eagerly awaited, ambitious restorations in UK history. Now managed under the watchful eye of Fairmont Hotels and Resorts, the restoration, which began in 2007, has seen the entire building lovingly remodelled, from the iconic entrance to the 268 guestrooms and suites with new interiors by world-renowned designer Pierre Yves-Rochon. The new look seamlessly blends elements of the original and new while remaining true to the spirit of the hotel's two main design aesthetics, Edwardian and Art Deco. Within the Thames Foyer, the re-introduction of a winter garden gazebo beneath an ornate glass dome provides the perfect ambience for afternoon tea. In addition, there is River Restaurant, offering a Modern French menu under Chef de Cuisine Ryan Murphy while the Savoy Grill has just returned under the operation of Gordon Ramsay Holdings with Chef Patron, Stuart Gillies. Service couldn't get more quintessentially English: a band of butlers offering 24-7 attention.

Q INSIDER: It was ever thus: The Savoy is one of the most exciting places in London to drink and dine. The world-famous American Bar has been newly restored (but still serves its famous 'White Lady' cocktail). New to the hotel is the Beaufort Bar, a glamorous Art Deco bar, and Savoy Tea, a bijou teashop selling Savoy tea and fresh patisserie.

THE ATHENAEUM

LONDON, ENGLAND. COORDINATES – N 51° 30.274, W 000° 08.843

The five – star Athenaeum overlooks leafy Green Park, Buckingham Palace and is a stroll to chic shops and West End theatres. It is contemporary, creative and friendly, boasting a stunning 'Living Wall' exterior of rich evergreen foliage (a subtle piece of artwork, designed by Patric Blanc that truly sets the building apart). This beautiful setting is like a home from home in London, a family-owned hotel with only 156 rooms, suites and apartments. Each finishing touch is designed for relaxation and convenience – guests can stay put and enjoy the state-of-the-art Bose docking stations for iPods in every room, large plasma screens and free WiFi. The onus is on making each guest feel as comfortable as possible and it's hard to resist the selection of pay-per-view movies or complimentary mini-bars stocked with soft drinks and snacks. Guests also have access to the hotel spa. The all-day restaurant looks as gorgeous as the food; the cosy Whisky Bar serves up everything your heart desires, and experts will urge you to try their award – winning Afternoon Tea.

Q INSIDER: The Athenaeum provides a dedicated 'Kids Concierge' service, a special weekend playroom, and also offers a nanny service.

For booking enquiries contact Quintessentially Travel
Email: reserve@quintessentiallytravel.com, Tel: +44 (0)845 224 6915

BROWN'S HOTEL

LONDON, ENGLAND. COORDINATES – N 51° 30.488, W 000° 08.694

Rocco Forte's Brown's Hotel has possibly the most prestigious address London has to offer – on Albemarle Street in the heart of Mayfair, around the corner from Bond Street's shopping, a five-minute walk to the Royal Academy, and within walking distance of theatreland. Yet despite this positioning at the capital's buzzing heart, Brown's maintains the most intimate of atmospheres. Each room and suite is individually furnished with attention given to the minutiae that make the difference, from luxurious fabrics to carefully selected modern artworks and books. The Donovan Bar quietly hums with the local art and fashion crowd while HIX at The Albemarle, overseen by super-chef Mark Hix, marks the apotheosis of great British cooking (the set menu changes daily to keep the coterie of regulars on their toes). With The English Tea Room voted 'Top [ ] on Afternoon Tea 2009' by The Tea Guild, it's easy to see why Brown's merits its description as an institution among London five-star hotels. For a full taste of this pedigree, book The Kipling Suite where the eponymous novelist was inspired to pen many of his tales.

Q INSIDER: The 'Rocco Forte Suite Experience' includes a wide choice of bed linen, breakfast, a packing and unpacking service, daily gifts, complimentary internet, movies on demand and use of a mobile phone pre-programmed to connect at the press of a button to the hotel concierge.

For booking enquiries contact Quintessentially Travel
Email: reserve@quintessentiallytravel.com, Tel: +44 (0)845 224 6915

THE HALKIN

LONDON, ENGLAND. COORDINATES – N 51° 30.044, W 000° 09.131

The Halkin is a haven in the heart of London's Georgian Belgravia. It promises discreet luxury where service is efficient and intimacy matters. Yet the look is elegantly contemporary, and the boutique-size (24 rooms and 1? suites) remains enduringly appealing. It is a place to relax and be waited on, to sleep and be reinvigorated, where serenity is proved the essence of the hotel experience. Bespoke Italian design is combined with subtle nuances of Oriental influence. Comfort is fundamental with Egyptian linens of the highest thread-count, oversized beds, soft carpets and warm wood panelling as well as some of the largest bathrooms in London. The Halkin's rooms are equipped with the most up-to-date technological features including interactive ETV and complimentary WiFi. Fo the discerning gourmet, nahm at The Halkin offers delectable eastern cuisine in Europe's first Michelin-starred Tha restaurant from Australian chef David Thompson.

Q INSIDER: The Halkin Bar now offers a 'Flights of Wine' menu showcasing a selection of interesting wine pairings Each 'flights' consists of three 125ml glasses of wine. Choices include a 'Riesling Flight', 'Alsatian Flight' and a 'Mystery flight'. Prices start from £17 per 'Flight' and include a selection of light bites.

GRAND-HÔTEL DU CAP-FERRAT

SAINT – JEAN CAP – FERRAT, FRANCE
COORDINATES – N 43° 40.618, E 007° 19.887

The Grand-Hôtel du Cap-Ferrat is one of those Côte d'Azur addresses rich in myth. There is the dream location on the tip of the Cap – Ferrat peninsula. True to this glamorous, Gatsby-esque neck-of-the-woods, the architecture is classic Belle Epoque flanked by 17 acres of gardens and pinewood. The hotel features some 49 rooms and suites in the historical building, plus 24 additional guestrooms in a new extension including eight suites, which are the only five-star suites in France with private swimming pools and sea views. There is also a spacious new spa. Chef Didier Aniès, Meilleur Ouvrier de France, continues to head up Michelin-starred restaurant Le Cap, the hotel's gourmet fixture, which in July and August features Friday fireworks on the terraces. And as ever, the pool is the pièce de résistance: infinity-edged and Olympic-sized.

Q INSIDER: The Villa Rose Pierre is a four-bedroom palace in a 2.5 acre private park with a swimming pool, clay tennis court, games room, sauna, gym and seven dedicated staff. You can rent it on a monthly basis in high and mid-season, and weekly in low season.

For booking enquiries contact Quintessentially Travel
Email: reserve@quintessentiallytravel.com, Tel: +44 (0)845 224 6915

RITZ PARIS

PARIS, FRANCE. COORDINATES – N 48° 52.087, E 002° 19.734

The legend of the Ritz Paris started with Cesar Ritz. When he opened it in 1898, he revolutionised the hotel business. Next came Mohamed Al Fayed and his family. In 1979, he acquired the Ritz Paris and set out to restore all of its prestige. Anybody who is anyone has stayed over the years, from Hemingway to Proust, Wilde and Capote. It is a stellar roll-call that continues with the private apartment concept that Ritz developed and which Mademoiselle Chanel best described; she lived in the hotel for more than 35 years and declared: "For me, The Ritz is home". Located on the elegant Place Vendôme, the hotel has 103 superbly appointed rooms and 56 suites as well as the renowned Ecole Ritz Escoffier cooking school, the two Michelin-starred gastronomic restaurant L'Espadon, three hotel bars, an in-house swimming pool and six-hole putting green.

Q INSIDER: If there is one thing you must not miss on any account during your stay, it's a visit to the Hemingway Bar. This upscale watering hole - where the author famously sipped single malts - is one of the most celebrated spots in Paris that is brimming with character, Old World charm and plenty of glamour.

HOTEL PLAZA ATHÉNÉE PARIS

PARIS, FRANCE. COORDINATES – N 48° 51.971, E 002° 18.263

Behind the red-geranium façade of Hôtel Plaza Athénée on Avenue Montaigne lies a true haven of peace. Virginia creepers adorn the beautiful inner courtyard throughout the summer while glistening pine trees and an ice-rink create a magical wonderland scene during winter. Decorated in a classical or Art Deco style, the apartments reflect the refinement of Paris integrated with state-of-the-art technology. The Eiffel Tower Penthouses, true Parisian apartments, offer a staggering view on the Eiffel Tower. Take a relaxing break at Dior Institut at the Plaza Athénée, the first truly Parisian House of Beauty with five treatments rooms, a fitness suite, steam room and sauna. Continue the evening in the haute cuisine restaurant, Alain Ducasse at the Plaza Athénée, and sip one of the audacious and creative cocktails at the Bar. Entirely designed by Patrick Jouin, the Bar combines classic and modern, and continually astonishes the A-list of Parisian beauties who gather here steps from the city's fashion houses.

Q INSIDER: A staggering 550 staff members anticipate every need. Make the most of all this luxury, from the two shoe-shines (Q recommends the exclusive Berlutti) to a wine cellar of 35,000 bottles.

HOTEL LE MEURICE

PARIS, FRANCE. COORDINATES – N 48° 51.908, E 002° 19.679

It has a stellar location, opposite the Tuileries Garden, between Place de la Concorde and the Musée du Louvre. It has a formidable history, Le Meurice operating as one of the great palace hotels of Paris since 1835. And it's got a shot of the new, the hotel experiencing huge investment in recent years. Not only does this mean a highly polished guest experience – seamless service that is hard to beat in Paris – but also an avant garde, creative energy that can only belong to France. Gourmet three-star cuisine is by Yannick Alléno, among France's most celebrated young chefs, his whimsical twists on traditional dishes perfectly reflecting the daring that occasionally shows its face at Le Meurice (Bar 228, for instance, and the newly-styled dining room, by Philippe Starck).

Q INSIDER: Make time for the Spa Valmont – a tranquil idyll with natural accents in marble, wood, stone and glass. The Valmont anti-aging treatments are among a Frenchwoman's more closely guarded beauty secrets.

For booking enquiries contact Quintessentially Travel
Email: reserve@quintessentiallytravel.com, Tel: +44 (0)845 224 6915

LE ROYAL MONCEAU
RAFFLES PARIS

PARIS, FRANCE. COORDINATES – N 48° 52.542, E 002° 18.007

The refurbishment of Le Royal Monceau, Raffles Paris is a showpiece of luxury hotel design from Philippe Starck. While aiming to attract the artistic, intellectual types who adored this classic palace in the 1930s, you can also expect a whole new kind of global nomad following the designer's redo of this Right Bank fixture just steps from the Champs Elysées. The 40s-style interiors break away from convention with the odd acoustic guitar – subtle, playful notes that bring this grand dame bang up to date. Dining choices include fine Italian cuisine at Il Carpaccio, French cuisine at La Cuisine, and cocktails recalling the sparkling society parties of the 1930s at Le Bar Long. Pastry chef Pierre Herme, whom Vogue magazine dubbed 'the Picasso of pastry' creates the hotel's desserts and pastries. There's a hotel cinema (a first for Paris), a vast spa by Clarins, a 26m-long pool and fully staffed kids' club.

Q INSIDER: If Paris doesn't already offer a surfeit of attractions to art lovers, then add this to the mix: the hotel boasts its own contemporary arts bookstore with television screens beaming live feeds from art auctions. There is also an 'Art Concierge'.

LA RÉSERVE PARIS
APARTMENTS

PARIS, FRANCE. COORDINATES – N 48° 51.800, E 002° 17.168

La Réserve has chosen Paris, the City of Light, as the setting for its residential jewel in the prime location of the Place du Trocadéro, in the supremely chic 16th arrondissement. La Réserve Paris Apartments offers a secure, private realm with 10 apartments ranging from 150 to 300 square metres featuring a spectacular view of the Eiffel Tower. Technological comfort rounds off the splendour of Rémi Tessier's contemporary design. Every detail has been carefully thought out to make each second of your stay perfect with an extensive range of à la carte residential services, a concierge worthy of a five-star property, a housekeeper, valet parking and personal home-chef. The most elegant neighbourhood in the French capital is the ideal setting in which to indulge in La Réserve's art of living and enjoy all that Paris has to offer, be it for a romantic weekend or a full-length stay.

Q INSIDER: For those seeking that little piece of private heaven within the city there's no need to even leave the Residence. Celebrated horticulturalist and landscape gardener, Jean – Christophe Stoerkel has joined forces with Daniel Besneux to create a haven that beautifully reflects the gardens at the foot of the Eiffel Tower.

For booking enquiries contact Quintessentially Travel
Email: reserve@quintessentiallytravel.com, Tel: +44 (0)845 224 6915

LA RÉSERVE RAMATUELLE HOTEL SPA & VILLAS

CÔTE D'AZUR, FRANCE. COORDINATES – N 43° 11.757, E 006° 39.133

Ideally located just minutes from the village of Saint Tropez and overlooking the Mediterranean, la Réserve Ramatuelle is a world apart, suspended between earth and sky in exquisite fusion with an exceptional natural environment. Internationally renowned architect Jean-Michel Wilmotte designed La Réserve Ramatuelle Hotel & Spa, harmoniously integrated into the private domain of the La Réserve Ramatuelle rental villas. There are 23 rooms and suites catering to the comfort of a handful of privileged people. A 1000 sq m spa is dedicated to improving long-term well-being and focuses on personalised treatments involving nutrition, relaxation sessions and physical activities. Guests can enjoy an indoor pool with a jet lane, an outdoor pool (complete with a pool house) and a steam bath. The bar and restaurant serve up deliciously healthy dishes from the region, all guaranteed to tickle the most discerning taste buds in this beautiful secret refuge.

Q INSIDER: The La Réserve Ramatuelle domain includes 12 villas for rent, each with its own pool and private garden. All face the sea and feature from four to six bedrooms. What makes them stand apart is the fact they come with hotel-level services, as per your requirements: a home-chef, butler, babysitting, beauty and spa therapists and even personal trainers.

LE NEGRESCO

NICE, FRANCE. COORDINATES – N 43° 41.663, E 007° 15.492

The majestic Negresco, a 125-room palace-hotel overlooking that world-famous stretch of seafront Promenade that gives Nice its heritage and glamour, is a place to be pampered, summer or winter, in the intimate surroundings of a hotel elaborately decorated by the resident owner, Mme Augier. What's more, Negresco has never looked better following a recent six – month closure to renovate suites and add new VIP services. The hotel's private beach, Le Neptune, lies just in front of the hotel, while numerous museums and theatres; Cannes, Monte Carlo and picturesque hilltop villages are all located nearby. The old town of Nice, sequestering exceptional restaurants, is a 15-minute walk. In the evenings, enjoy a glass of Champagne in Le Relais cocktail bar before dining in the sophisticated one Michelin-starred restaurant, Le Chantecler. For a light meal or snack, the hotel's second restaurant, La Rotonde, stays open all day where chef Jean-Denis Rieubland works small miracles using Mediterranean market-fresh vegetables and locally caught fish.

Q INSIDER: At a bargain rate of 17 euros per day, guests can bring their dogs. Your little pooch will be provided with his own rug and water bowl and be taken out for exercise along that dramatic Promenade. Also Le Negresco will offer readers a VIP treatment for any booking from the seaview room category.

For booking enquiries contact Quintessentially Travel
Email: reserve@quintessentiallytravel.com, Tel: +44 (0)845 224 6915

CHÂTEAU DE BAGNOLS

BAGNOLS, FRANCE. COORDINATES – N 45° 53.472, E 004° 40.054

Dating from the 13th century, you've got all the dreamscape elements: the original dry moat, towers and a dramatic entrance across a drawbridge. Yet the owner hasn't chosen to be greedy and stuff in as many rooms as possible. Instead you will find just 21 rooms and suites and a Michelin-starred restaurant, Salle des Gardes, serving regional cuisine. The interior detail has been painstakingly restored, and includes Renaissance wall and ceiling paintings. After all, this is not only a hotel, but also one of the country's major historical monuments set within striking gardens. These include a lavender walk, some 140 cherry trees and wide-canopied, 100-year-old limes.

Q INSIDER: Wine-buffs will want to ask the hotel for a special vineyard tour which can also include a hot air balloon flight over the famous Beaujolais hills.

For booking enquiries contact Quintessentially Travel
Email: reserve@quintessentiallytravel.com, Tel: +44 (0)845 224 6915

GSTAAD PALACE

GSTAAD, SWITZERLAND. COORDINATES – N 46° 28.484, E 7° 17.209

The Gstaad Palace hotel is indivisible from the history of this great Swiss ski resort where the likes of Gunther Sachs and Brigitte Bardot used to sashay down the slopes. To this day, this family-owned, 104-room resort is still among the benchmarks for Europe's other grand dame mountain hotels. And look up to it you must, for the palace occupies a commanding mountaintop position overlooking the chocolate-box village where the sound of sleighbells rings through the streets (the best view of the valley spread is from the three-bedroom Penthouse – the first ever built in an Alpine resort). Service, from concierge through to spa therapist, is as good as you'd expect in a country where the best hotel staff in the world receive their formative training. There are five restaurants offering traditional Swiss dishes, savoury grill specialties, an exceptional Italian menu and exquisite gourmet cuisine. Other musts are a drink at the lobby bar and a twirl in the resort's famous GreenGo nightclub.

Q INSIDER: If you tire of skiing, there's an 1800sq m Palace Spa with eight treatment rooms, a private spa suite, saunas and steam bath, relaxation areas with incredible views, an indoor pool and outdoor pool with Jacuzzi, a state-of-the-art gym, Pilates studio and a unique hammam experience.

BEAU-RIVAGE PALACE

LAUSANNE, SWITZERLAND. COORDINATES – N 46° 30.490, E 006° 37.798

For nearly 150 years, Lake Geneva has reflected the dazzling lights of the Beau–Rivage Palace in the city of Lausanne. Completely renovated, this Belle Epoque building commands breathtaking Alpine views. Flick through the Beau-Rivage Palace's guestbook and you will find Coco Chanel, Gary Cooper and Noel Coward (who immortalised the hotel in 'A Song at Twilight').
The 168 guest rooms and suites are richly appointed and offer the utmost in elegance and comfort. The palace's four restaurants include the two Michelin-starred Anne-Sophie Pic at Beau-Rivage Palace, opened in spring 2009. The Café Beau-Rivage serves brasserie-style fare in sophisticated surroundings, with a large terrace facing the lake, while sushi restaurant Miyako Lausanne offers on-the-spot Japanese treasures. At the end of the day, the Bar provides a relaxed atmosphere with live music.

Q INSIDER: Cinq Mondes Spa is a 15,000sq ft spa offering a variety of massages, from Balinese to Taoist, as well as pampering, anti-ageing and restorative treatments, all of which are delivered to those exacting Swiss standards. There is also an indoor and outdoor pool as well as tennis courts.

For booking enquiries contact Quintessentially Travel
Email: reserve@quintessentiallytravel.com, Tel: +44 (0)845 224 6915

LA RÉSERVE GENÈVE HOTEL & SPA

GENÈVE, SWITZERLAND. COORDINATES – N 46° 15.114, E 006° 09.021

La Réserve Genève, Hotel and Spa is blissfully refreshing, a chic, contemporary-styled hotel. Designed by star designer, Jacques Garcia, he wittily re-interprets the idea of an African reserve with interiors that include a tented restaurant, woven rattan walls and an elephant sculpture in the lobby with parrots nestling in lampshades. There are 102 rooms including 17 suites. Most have a terrace or balcony overlooking the hotel's gardens and Lake Geneva beyond. La Réserve is also home to one of the most stylish bars in Geneva, Le Bar, with a live DJ each evening. Le Loti serves French food. Le Tsé-Fung specialises in opulent Chinese cuisine with two private rooms recommended for events.

Q INSIDER: La Réserve's all-white spa with a glorious pool is comprehensive, offering personalised programs. They tackle age prevention, stress and weight in meaningful ways, making use of La Réserve's full gamut of specialists.

HÔTEL DES TROIS COURONNES

VEVEY, SWITZERLAND. COORDINATES – N 46° 27.510, E 006° 50.883

Just a 50-minute drive from Geneva airport, between the lakeside towns of Montreux and Lausanne, lies Hôtel des Trois Couronnes on the shores of Lake Geneva, facing the Alps. Dating from 1842, this one-time feudal castle is among Switzerland's great hotels, a neo–classical beauty that has hosted grandees from Tsarinas to the Shah of Persia. They've all passed through – composers, artists, literary greats – and in the new era, an international tribe of discerning, spa-focused travellers. For this is also a hotel that defines contemporary luxury living, Hôtel des Trois Couronnes recently refurbished with striking silk-dressed rooms and suites (all with fireplaces). It also has a comprehensive modern spa. Combined with the setting, it's a great place to smooth out the wrinkles while feasting on inventive French cuisine that can be enjoyed on a lakeside terrace in summer. The spa is considered one of the best in Switzerland with an indoor pool with underwater music, aqua relaxation, a sauna, steam bath, fitness room, gym classes as well as a Joëlle Ciocco Epidermiologic Centre. All-inclusive packages and special offers are offered for stays – so be sure to ask at the time of booking.

Q INSIDER: As if we weren't spoilt enough – watch out for the stunning Puressens Destination Spa launching in July 2011. Based on the three fundamental pillars of mind, body and soul, it promises to take us straight to relaxation heaven.

For booking enquiries contact Quintessentially Travel
Email: reserve@quintessentiallytravel.com, Tel: +44 (0)845 224 6915

GRAND HOTEL
LES TROIS ROIS

BASEL, SWITZERLAND. COORDINATES – N 47° 33.629, E 007° 35.254

Grand Hotel Les Trois Rois in the Swiss town of Basel sits at the crossroads of three countries; located just a few miles from the French and German border, it makes a great base for day excursions to the villages of the Alsace in France or Germany's fairytale Black Forest. It also has one foot in the old and one foot in the new; the hotel, which dates from 1681, has recently been completely renovated and its historic structure restored with meticulous attention to detail. The perfect size for a mini-grand hotel, Les Trois Rois is made up of 101 rooms and suites stuffed with antique furniture and works of art. Look out from the window and it gets even better, with views of the Rhine and Basel's old town. Guests can choose between the spectacular two-star Michelin restaurant Cheval Blanc with Switzerland's chef of the year 2011 Peter Knogl and its exclusive waterside terrace, the French Brasserie or Chez Donati, a stylish Italian eatery serving homemade pasta.

Q INSIDER: The glamorous Suite Les Trois Rois, a heaven of Art Nouveau design, occupies the top floor of the historic building. The highlight is its rooftop terrace – one of the highest spots in Basel's city centre – with its private sauna and whirlpool.

DO & CO HOTEL VIENNA

VIENNA, AUSTRIA. COORDINATES – N 48° 12.502, E 016° 22.290

You know you're onto something when the hotel bar and restaurant is packed with locals. Such is the story of DO & CO Hotel Vienna, a venue well regarded among the Viennese for the lively ONYX bar and the multicultural cuisine at DO & CO Stephansplatz restaurant on the hotel's rooftop. Sure the central location helps – in the city's heart bang opposite the landmark St. Stephen's Cathedral. The hotel occupies six floors of the futuristic Haas Haus with 43 rooms and suites. Throughout, only the finest materials grace interiors, from teak to travertine stone floors and furniture made from Turkish leather. In-room technology is bang on trend, with Bang & Olufsen televisions, iPod docking stations and Ninetendo Wii consoles. The bathroom amenities find their way into most guests' bags; suffice to say they are made by Etro.

Q INSIDER: In a building designed by Pritzker-prize winner Hans Hollein, you can expect a few design surprises to match the drama of the steel-and-glass exterior. Q's favourite? The 2 m sq. bathrooms to all 43 cone-shaped guestrooms.

GRAND HOTEL TREMEZZO

LAKE COMO, ITALY. COORDINATES – N 45° 59.088, E 009° 13.714

In the shadow of the snow-covered Rhaetian Alps and hemmed in on both sides by steep, verdant hillsides, Lake Como is the most spectacular of the three major lakes in Northern Italy. Built in 1910, the Belle Epoque Grand Hotel Tremezzo is a Lake Como landmark – a vintage symbol of Italian hospitality and place-to-be to enjoy the flavour of real vacation (Greta Garbo famously declared that she couldn't wait to get back to the happy, sunny Tremezzo in the 1932 film, Grand Hotel). With soul-stirring views of the lake – the hotel has 100 windows overlooking the blue waters or flowering greenery of the garden – you will find the romance and exclusivity many hotels promise but few deliver. The mix of contemporary flair and old-time values is discernible in the 88 elegant rooms, two suites and lakefront classic-style lido with a private Venetian lancia boat. There are three breathtaking pools (one floating on the lake, one hidden in the park, one indoor infinity), the panoramic 'T Spa' and a two-acre park with a floodlit clay tennis court.

Q INSIDER: Italian cuisine is deservedly famous and you can explore its numerous highlights and specialities at the Tremezzo's five different restaurants and snack bars. You'll be spoilt for choice – a star chef of Italian cuisine wowing guests with exciting culinary delights.

For booking enquiries contact Quintessentially Travel
Email: reserve@quintessentiallytravel.com, Tel: +44 (0)845 224 6915

GRAND HOTEL
A VILLA FELTRINELLI

GARGNANO, ITALY. COORDINATES – N 45° 41.591, E 010° 40.125

Within an easy two-to three-hour drive of Milan on the banks of Lake Garda you will find Villa Feltrinelli. This is one of the most perfect 'baby grand' hotels in all Europe. Detail is everything. With just 21 rooms in total – 13 formal suites in the 19th-century villa, with nine more rustic-contemporary rooms occupying the three cottages and boat house – there is the time to ensure no request, however small, is overlooked. Rooms feature personal touches such as silver-framed black-and-white photos, hand-printed Venetian paper desk sets and stationery containers; minibar items are complimentary, as well as personal laundry, unpacking services and Acqua di Parma toiletries. Like a private home, guests can order food at anytime and be served anywhere whether it's around the croquet lawn during an impromptu match with other guests, or beneath the sweet-smelling magnolias. There is an outdoor pool, your very own private access to the property's lake-side, and enough antiques to make Christies green with envy.

Q INSIDER: For those who want the private feel of a villa but with round-the-clock hotel services, impeccable food and spoken English, then Villa Feltrinelli is the ideal match (and in a part of the world where regular villas, however grand their history, can still suffer from inattentive housekeeping).

For booking enquiries contact Quintessentially Travel
Email: reserve@quintessentiallytravel.com, Tel: +44 (0)845 224 6915

ALPENPALACE DELUXE HOTEL & SPA RESORT

VALLE AURINA, ITALY. COORDINATES – N 46° 57.767, E 011° 55.294

Alpenpalace, located in the heart of the South Tyrol's Ahrn Valley, is the sort of retreat you dream about when you want to get away from it all, summer or winter (the hotel is within three kilometers of the Klausberg and Speikboden ski areas). The point is not only the natural surroundings – the Dolomites were recently added to the UNESCO World Heritage List – but the spa. This 2000sq m space is a testament to modern Alpine style and features an indoor pool with massage beds, an outdoor pool with air massage, a Tyrolean sauna, herbal bath, steam bath, laconium, a beauty farm featuring La Prairie treatments, and numerous resting areas – all with views of the resort's seven-acre park and beyond that, the mighty South Tyrolean Alps. The culinary offering includes local Italian and international specialties, as well as a vast buffet area, a buzzy bar and expansive sun terrace.

Q INSIDER: The new Jardin Suite with her natural antique wood interiors, sunny garden and terrace is the best room of all to take in the Ahrntaler mountain panorama.

SAVOIA EXCELSIOR PALACE

TRIESTE, ITALY. COORDINATES – N 45° 38.972, E 013° 45.927

The Savoia Excelsior Palace is rich in history and location. Overlooking the Adriatic in beautiful Trieste, this grand hotel's turn-of-the-20th-century architecture dates back to the glories of the Austro-Hungarian Empire. Following a renovation completed mid-2009, the 142-room hotel has never looked better. New interiors mix contemporary Italian design with the hotel's elegant Mittle-European style. The Savoy Lounge features a majestic shell-shaped ceiling. The Savoy Restaurant and Le Rive Bar, located off the lobby, offer majestic views over the gulf of Trieste. The new winter garden, which also serves as the hotel's library, hits a different note again, this resolutely contemporary space breaking away from the more classical feel of the main lobby where the great and good like to gather. Just be sure to get out and explore. Trieste sequesters not just history, but some of the best unsung dining experiences in Europe.

Q INSIDER: Book a room facing the Gulf of Trieste; these rooms have great terraces as well as peerless views of the Adriatic and the famous Castello di Miramare.

PARK HYATT MILAN

MILAN, ITALY. COORDINATES – N 45° 27.938, E 9° 11.333

Park Hyatt Milan is a contemporary design hotel in a 19th-century building steps from the Duomo and overlooking the Galleria Vittorio Emanuele. So yes, you couldn't do better for a city centre location, nor for the concentration of history, culture and shopping in a single block. This is also the kind of hotel non-residents adore; specifically, the Cupola Lobby Lounge offering an all-day menu and tasty sunday brunch. The Park Bar also buzzes with locals as does The Park Restaurant, a contemporary Italian focusing on seasonal highlights. But still, this remains a discreet address that holds its true pleasures close – the fabulously private 108 guestrooms and suites designed by Ed Tuttle. The rooms are bathed in natural light and come fully equipped with walk-in closets and extra large bathrooms with deep soaking baths and octagonal rain showers.

Q INSIDER: If you're in town for Fashion Week, don't think about booking the details later. The hotel's much-loved spa is a nugget of gold, offering a whirlpool, steam bath, a fully-geared gym, two rooms for a variety of holistic beauty treatments and a private spa room for couples.

BULGARI HOTEL MILANO

MILAN, ITALY. COORDINATES – N 45° 28.227, E 009° 11.400

You would struggle do better than the Bulgari Hotel Milano's central address – a five-minute walk from Via Monte Napoleone, which is the city's main shopping drag, and 10 minutes from La Scala opera house. Yet you benefit from a great lung of greenery – adjacent to 4,000 square metres of botanical garden. The rooms blend modern design, high technology features and lavish materials including oak and bronze. Bathrooms are bedecked in Zimbabwean and travertine marble, with a gold mesh screen dividing the space from the bedroom. Some rooms offer teakwood balconies with views of the garden below. There is a casual but elegant outdoor terrace restaurant, which bustles with the Milanese in summer, as well as an indoor alternative and bar. The SPA & Wellness Centre has an indoor pool with steam bath, five treatment rooms and a personal trainer.

Q INSIDER: The Bulgari offers complimentary WiFi. If this is standard where you come from, Sunday brunch at the Bulgari Hotel is anything but. The Milanese flock in at weekends, salivating over the perfectly simple spaghetti with tomato sauce from chef Elio Sironi.

For booking enquiries contact Quintessentially Travel
Email: reserve@quintessentiallytravel.com, Tel: +44 (0)845 224 6915

L'ALBERETA RELAIS
& CHATEAUX

ERBUSCO, ITALY. COORDINATES – N 45° 33.751, E 9° 58.980

Family-owned L'Albereta seems to have it all: a stunning location in Italy's Franciacorta region, a serious Espace Vitalité Henri Chenot spa, cuisine from Gualtiero Marchesi – the first restaurant in Italy to ever receive the three-star rating from Michelin – and envy-creating history. L'Albereta consists of five buildings: the original villa with the Bellavista tower, the new Lake View Tower, the farmhouse with its portico, the Contadi Castaldi Tower and the adjoining Casa Leone. In all there are 57 rooms and suites. Elegant and discreet, you come here to get away from it all, to feel better in the trusted hands of expert therapists while indulging (just a little) in exceptional local wines (the vineyards of Bellavista and Contadi Castaldi are on L'Albereta's doorstep). Further facilities include an indoor swimming pool with Jacuzzi, a gym, billiard room, tennis court and fitness path.

Q INSIDER: The exclusive Cabriolet Suite is located at the top of the Lake View Tower. While you are comfortably relaxed on the bed, push a button and the entire roof of the room, including the tiles and ridge caps, retract on moving rails to reveal the sky.

For booking enquiries contact Quintessentially Travel
Email: reserve@quintessentiallytravel.com, Tel: +44 (0)845 224 6915

IL PELLICANO HOTEL

GROSSETO, ITALY. COORDINATES – N 42° 22.430, E 11° 11.234

Il Pellicano was born of a love story – built in memory of Pelican Point, the Californian promontory where the British army pilot, Michael Graham, and the American jetsetter, Patsy Daszel, first met in the 1940s. When they chose to build their own European retreat, they opted for this spot overlooking the cliffs on Tuscany's Monte Argentario in the undiscovered Maremma region. Now owned by an Italian, Roberto Scio, this world-known hotel, which once welcomed everyone from Gianni Agnelli to Charlie Chaplin, remains an intimate, classy experience. The property consists of 35 rooms and 15 suites spread over 7000 square metres of vegetation. It is also a gourmet destination with a two Michelin-star restaurant and a typical Tuscan 'all'aperto' grill for high season. The Pelliclub health and beauty centre offers a wide range of treatments. There is a private beach, heated saltwater pool, tennis court and golf a five-minute drive away.

Q INSIDER: Take advantage of the Master Deluxe Suite featuring a private pool. Alternatively, rent one of the cottages located in Il Pellicano's grounds. This allows you the villa experience with hotel services attached – and is ideal for family reunions.

For booking enquiries contact Quintessentially Travel
Email: reserve@quintessentiallytravel.com, Tel: +44 (0)845 224 6915

CASTIGLION DEL BOSCO

SIENA, ITALY. COORDINATES – N 43° 05.035, E 011° 25.305

Castiglion del Bosco is a magnificent 450-acre Brunello winemaking estate dating back to the Middle Ages. The estate lies within the UNESCO-listed Val d'Orcia Natural Park, and boasts an ancient chapel with frescoes by Sienese master Pietro Lorenzetti. But today the handsome Borgo (village) at the centre of the property also hosts an intimate, effortlessly chic 23-room hotel that will surprise even the seasoned aesthete and Italy addict. In addition to the hotel suites, nine villas are scattered around the grounds, all with private heated pools. Attention to detail is the watchword here: from the carefully selected Tuscan products in the Borgo's on-site Negozio to the weight of the curtains and the stitching on the staff uniforms, everything is spot on. The estate also offers a wide range of sporting facilities, including a world-class golf course (to be completed in 2011), a state-of-the-art fitness centre, tennis and bocce courts and miles of hiking, running and mountain bike-trails. There is a Culinary Academy, gourmet restaurant, a relaxed osteria, a kitchen garden and an infinity pool with views that will blow your mind.

Q INSIDER: The Daniela Steiner spa is right in the heart of the Borgo. This haven of good health and wellbeing distills all the goodness of the Tuscan countryside in its beauty and

THE ST. REGIS GRAND HOTEL, ROME

ROME, ITALY. COORDINATES – N 41° 54.238, E 12° 29.689

From the outside, The St. Regis Grand Hotel, Rome looks more like a noble residence than hotel. This is in sympathy with its location in the city's heart, within walking distance of the Spanish Steps, Trevi Fountain and Via Veneto. The Colosseum, Roman Forum, Piazza Navona and stores of Via Condotti are also nearby. It was originally opened in 1894 by Cesar Ritz as the city's first luxury hotel; in December 1999 it underwent a $35 million dollar renovation. Furniture is a combination of styles including Empire, Regency and Louis XV. Every guestroom has its own unique identity, each fresco depicting a significant ruin, monument or area of the city. The Bottega Veneta is the newest suite and Q's tip; it is designed by Tomas Maier with three bedrooms, a living room with a fireplace, the whole furnished with select pieces from the Bottega Veneta home collection.

INSIDER If the 24/7 St. Regis butlers aren't enough to keep you happy, swing by the hotel's highly regarded Vivendo restaurant as well as the 'di...Vino' wine cellar beneath. The space comprises stones from the Emperor Diocletian's Roman baths, located just a few steps from the hotel.

ROMEO HOTEL

NAPLES, ITALY. COORDINATES – N 40° 50.438, E 014° 15.350

Facing the Gulf of Naples, Romeo Hotel is a perfect synthesis of Italian craftsmanship and international contemporary design. Featuring pieces by Antonio Citterio and Philippe Starck, the hotel combines sea and city, relaxed style and polished service. With a city centre location you are only a short walk to the hydrofoils linking Naples to the islands of Capri and Ischia. Mount Vesuvius looms in the distance. The near neighbourhood is bright, lively and inimitably Mediterranean. There are 10 floors featuring some 84 rooms occupying a modern building designed by Studio Kenzo Tange, as well as a 700sq m spa and outdoor pool, a roof garden bar and a lounge for cigar tasting. Rooms are bedecked in furniture by B&B Italia, with beds laden in silk and Capri linen.

Q INSIDER: Despite being relatively small with 46 seats, Il Comandante, Romeo's gourmet restaurant, enjoys one of the biggest wine cellars in Italy with 750 different labels. For a fresh and modern taste of the sea, there is also Zero sushi bar.

For booking enquiries contact Quintessentially Travel
Email: reserve@quintessentiallytravel.com, Tel: +44 (0)845 224 6915

HOTEL CAESAR AUGUSTUS

ANACAPRI, ITALY. COORDINATES – N 40° 33.515, E 014° 13.387

At the turn of the 20th century, a noble Russian Prince claimed a cliff – top on Capri as his summer home to create one of the most dramatic mansions in all southern Italy. Now a hotel, the Caesar Augustus remains in the Signorini family – it is currently with the third generation – and has been lovingly restored into a 42-suite, 13-room property, with sparkling sea views from balconies and terraces. Perched 1000 feet above the water, you can see to the Bay of Naples, Mount Vesuvius, Sorrento and Ischia. The Terrace of Lucullus is the hotel's headline restaurant, where guests can enjoy the island gastronomy. Due to its location in the heart of Anacapri, you also benefit from numerous of the town's amenities, including tennis courts with professional trainers, shopping, spas and boat rentals. And all so easy; from Naples Port to Capri, it is a quick 45-minute hydrofoil journey.

Q INSIDER: Be sure to make time to venture onto the mainland and pad about the ruins of Pompeii – a Roman town drowned in 60ft drifts of volcanic ash in AD79. The city has been excavated over the years – and makes for a good hit of culture after all that Capri glamour.

For booking enquiries contact Quintessentially Travel
Email: reserve@quintessentiallytravel.com, Tel: +44 (0)845 224 6915

W BARCELONA

BARCELONA, SPAIN. COORDINATES – N 41° 22.133, E 002° 11.416

Located in a landmark building by star architect Ricardo Bofill, on the Nova Bocana (the 'new entrance') of the Port of Barcelona that connects the city's historic centre to the Mediterranean, W Barcelona is near the world-famous boardwalk La Barceloneta, the first-class restaurants of Port Vell, the pristine beaches and watersports of Puerto Olimpico, and a short stroll from the cafés, shops and nightlife of Barcelona's old town and Las Ramblas. W Barcelona is the only hotel in the city with direct access to the beach. Inspiring, iconic, innovative and influential, W Barcelona provides the ultimate in insider access to a world of 'Wow' With its unique mix of innovative design and passions around fashion, music and entertainment, you can expect contemporary restaurant concepts, glamorous nightlife experiences and stylish retail concepts

Q INSIDER: The hotel boasts Spain's first Bliss® Spa (an import from New York) a 'rooftop' bar from the Ignite group who created London's Boujis, and Wet® an infinity-edged pool flanked with cabanas.

For booking enquiries contact Quintessentially Travel
Email: reserve@quintessentiallytravel.com, Tel: +44 (0)845 224 6915

HOTEL HACIENDA
NA XAMENA

IBIZA, SPAIN. COORDINATES – N 39° 4.745, E 1° 25.209

Located only two hours away from every European capital, Ibiza's Hotel Hacienda is a quintessential luxury experience with distinct Spanish accents. The whitewashed architecture incorporates Arabic details and is combined with streams and waterfalls, patios and porticos. It's blissfully quiet, located in a nature reserve in the island's northeast with panoramic views of the cliffs of Na Xamena. From every room you can see the emerald sea. Yet you're only an easy 20-minute drive from the life of Ibiza Town. In the 65 rooms and suites, most of them equipped with a seaview Jacuzzi, you will be given the opportunity to get in harmony with your five senses. It will be your Renaissance. The Hotel shares a seven-hectare plot incorporating a Mediterranean pine wood and two kilometres of coast. So do the Ibiza thing: party and relax, comfortable in the knowledge you're staying at the right address for the island's hip insiders.

Q INSIDER: For the ultimate cellulite-busting detox, enjoy the Thalasso-trail of eight hydrotherapy baths (Las Cascadas Suspendidas), hanging on the cliff like the gardens of Semiramis. You'll need it after savouring the gourmet cuisine that makes perfect use of the incredible flavours of the Mediterranean spices.

For booking enquiries contact Quintessentially Travel
Email: reserve@quintessentiallytravel.com, Tel: +44 (0)845 224 6915

SHA WELLNESS

ALICANTE, SPAIN. COORDINATES – N 38° 33.588, W 000° 04.450

When SHA Wellness Clinic won the prestigious Condé Nast Traveller award for best 'Medical-Natural-Thermal Spa' within just 18 months of opening, the world sat up and listened. With rising expectations from an increasingly spa-literate clientele, SHA had made its mark for the simple reason it took wellness seriously, very seriously, in the way it combined holistic, eastern traditions with the latest medical advances. Privately owned by a man who saw his own life change for the better – much of this due to a dramatic macrobiotic diet – he hired the best specialists in the business to staff SHA with experts in genetic medicine, traditional Chinese medicine, nutrition psychology and more. The result is a super-mod, shiny-white contemporary wellness resort on the Spanish coast. Here the most demanding guests in the world can step back and enjoy therapeutic food and meaningful treatments on specific wellness programmes lasting from a long weekend to a month.

Q INSIDER: SHA's 14-day detox program is a big commitment, combining a macrobiotic diet with juice fasting, hydro-colon therapy and massage. It is ideal for those who invest the word with some gravitas, especially those wanting to clean up their systems after aggressive medical treatment or anyone suffering from uncharacteristic lethargy.

FINCA CORTESIN HOTEL GOLF & SPA

MÁLAGA, SPAIN. COORDINATES – N 36° 23.790, W 005° 13.467

Finca Cortesin Hotel Golf & Spa opened in the south of Spain in October 2008. Within a year it had found its pace, delivering a rare luxury experience in this much-visited region between Marbella and Sotogrande. Comprising 67 suites, private villas, a championship golf course and 7,010sq m spa, this is a place where you will want for nothing. Gourmands will adore the innovative Asian fusion cuisine at Schilo, the headline restaurant (the frozen grated foie gras layered on mirin-steeped carrot 'sushi' is stupendous) while those here simply to relax won't be able to get enough of the three vast pools (the main one, some 50 metres long, is flanked by an avenue of palms and scarlet-covered daybeds). The style combines an Andalucian aesthetic, including graceful interior courtyards and fountains, with contemporary detailing, all 67 suites lavishly appointed.

Q INSIDER: Finca Cortesin's golf course is one to watch. The exciting new Par-72 course designed by Cabell Robinson, has already secured numerous 'worldclass' converts. It will also be playing host to Volvo World Match Play in 2011 and 2012.

VILA JOYA
& JOY JUNG SPA

ALGARVE, PORTUGAL. COORDINATES – N 37 4.846, W 8 18.967

With a dramatic cliffside perch on the Algarve coast of southern Portugal, Vila Joya gets the sun and the drama of a justifiably popular golden strand of Europe. To do this privileged locale justice, each of the 20 rooms and suites is a one-off, meaning you can come back again and again and feel the freshness of the contemporary-classic-oriental design. More a boutique hotel than resort, Vila Joya boasts Portugal's only restaurant with two Michelin stars (successfully retained for more than a decade), with Chef Dieter Koschina's 'slow food' dishes enjoyed on a terrace restaurant with Atlantic views (on Thursday evenings the usual six-course menu ups to eight – a tip local cognoscenti keep close to their chests). The hotel wine cellar holds some 12,000 bottles. For the next-day detox, there's the Joy Jung Spa as well as more than 20 golf courses within a 30-minute reach.

Q INSIDER: The Xiringuito Beach Bar, a lounge bar located directly on the beach, is the perfect place to hang out day or night – and in summer, one of the buzziest spots on this stretch of the Algarve.

For booking enquiries contact Quintessentially Travel
Email: reserve@quintessentiallytravel.com, Tel: +44 (0)845 224 6915

MARTINHAL
BEACH RESORT & HOTEL

SAGRES, PORTUGAL. COORDINATES – N 37° 01.279, W 008° 55.594

The Algarve is having its moment right now – a fact that has much to do with the spring opening of the five-star Martinhal Beach Resort & Hotel. Appealing to families with high expectations of luxury, the resort has chosen its location perfectly: there's the stretch of sun-kissed sand, gentle waves for kid-friendly swimming, and flat coastal waters for watersports fanatics. The resort is made up of a 38-room boutique hotel as well as 132 one , two and three-bedroom 'village' houses set around a central 'village' square, which makes popping out for an ice-cream, getting a workout at the gym or meeting the children at the Kids Club an easy walk away. There's much to do, with a tennis academy, surfing, windsurfing, kite surfing, kayaking, diving, rock climbing, dolphin watching, deep-sea fishing and for some good old fashioned pampering, the resort's Finisterra Spa.

Q INSIDER: Even if the sun lounger is trying to persuade you otherwise, get out and explore. The resort is surrounded by the Costa Vicentina National Park, which is perfect for hiking and bike tours. Within a 10-minute drive are 11 beautiful beaches.

ANASSA

CYPRUS. COORDINATES – N 35° 2.608, E 32° 22.237

When the Anassa first arrived on Cyprus in the late 1990s, it rocked the Med – a fresh, modern, five-star beach resort that moved beyond the region's sprawling new-builds. It also opened a Thalassa Spa to beat the French at their own game (thalassotherapy, or seawater therapy, is why Biarritz girls don't get cellulite – or so they say). You know you're in Cyprus for the architecture speaks of the island's Byzantine roots. The experience is totally spoiling, with Emperor-sized villas and suites, some with private plunge pools and whirlpools on sea-facing terraces. There is a surfeit of facilities including a PADI dive school, powerboats, tennis and squash courts, a new 'Teen Club', kids club, crèche and 'Baby Go Lightly' service (you can pre-order all your baby requirements online before you travel) as well as four restaurants.

Q INSIDER: Even in November the weather can be balmy, which gives Cyprus the edge on the Med's competition.

For booking enquiries contact Quintessentially Travel
Email: reserve@quintessentiallytravel.com, Tel: +44 (0)845 224 6915

PORTO ZANTE
VILLAS & SPA

ZAKYNTHOS, GREECE. COORDINATES – N 37° 49.575, E 20° 50.901

Billed as 'Best Greek Hideaway Hotel' by Condé Nast Traveller magazine, Porto Zante Villas & Spa on the island of Zakynthos has a reputation that is fiercely protected. For there isn't room for everyone, this tiny villa-hotel with world-class villas on the beach, all with private pools, all with marble bathrooms and 24-hour hotel services. Zakynthos is the southernmost and third largest of the Ionian Islands – easily accessed from the mainland and thus boasting a 'crossroads' history (the Venetians, who ruled the island in the Middle Ages, named it 'Flower of the East'). On top of the views – that deep turquoise sea which can only belong to Greece – are super-chic interiors finished with selected pieces of Armani Casa, paintings by prominent Greek art the latest entertainment systems by Bang & Olufsen. There's a thalassotherapy spa (it's only right when you're this close to the sea) and Greek and Mediterranean cuisine at the Club House restaurant.

Q INSIDER: For a large group of up to 12 people, consider the Imperial Spa Villa with its private seawater pool, spa and private beach. This is a resort made for families. Yet it is also sophisticated, without feeling like it is overrun with kids.

For booking enquiries contact Quintessentially Travel
Email: reserve@quintessentiallytravel.com, Tel: +44 (0)845 224 6915

ELOUNDA GULF VILLAS & SUITES

CRETE, GREECE. COORDINATES – N 35 15.729, E 25 43.318

Award-winning Elounda Gulf Villas and Suites in Crete packs a big punch for a family-owned luxury villa-hotel. There are 10 suites and 18 one-to four-bedroom villas (including Spa Villas, each with a private gym room, sauna and steam bath). All villas offer private pools with Jacuzzis while the suites have access to the main seasonally-heated pool (also with a Jacuzzi). The property has been included for three consecutive years in Tatler magazine's '101 Best Hotels of the World', and is a member of the Small Luxury Hotels of the World. The à la carte Argo Restaurant serves delectable Mediterranean cuisine, Daphni Restaurant has gourmet dishes and The Argonauts is a glamorous lounge bar. Watersports include learning to dive in your own private villa pool, and there's Elixir Spa Gallery with gym, steam, sauna and massage room.

Q INSIDER: Every one of Elounda's vast accommodations has a stunning sea view of the Gulf of Mirabello. You feel like you're on a private villa vacation; the difference lies in the hybrid 'villa-hotel' concept designed to deliver services of the calibre associated with a top – tier luxury resort.

For booking enquiries contact Quintessentially Travel
Email: reserve@quintessentiallytravel.com, Tel: +44 (0)845 224 6915

ELOUNDA BEACH HOTEL

CRETE, GREECE. COORDINATES – N 35° 14.899 E 025° 43.902

Elounda is among the first beaches to roll off the tongue if you're talking luxury Crete. One of the jewels on the island's north-east stretch, this is where you find Elounda Beach Hotel – a perennial favourite for its mix of bungalows and suites with direct access to the sand, some rooms with private heated indoor and outdoor pools. There are two white private beaches lapped by the green Aegean, an outdoor heated seawater pool, a gym, thalassotherapy spa (with Henri Chenot treatments), five tennis courts (equipped for night play) and a comprehensive watersports centre. If that's still not enough to keep you happy, consider the gourmet panoply. Options range from Dionyssos with innovative Greek degustation menus, to Argonaut for lunchtime beachside grills, to Polynesian food and sushi. And for sheer originality, have a Google at the Yachting Club Villas...

Q INSIDER: For music and dancing in the middle of the sea, the Vegherra jetty bar is the spot to be. For more on the area's intriguing history, pack Victoria Hislop's bestselling novel, 'The Island' – an essential beach read for 2011.

For booking enquiries contact Quintessentially Travel
Email: reserve@quintessentiallytravel.com, Tel: +44 (0)845 224 6915

ELOUNDA
BAY PALACE HOTEL

CRETE, GREECE. COORDINATES – N 35° 15.136 E 025° 43.755

Elounda is probably the most famous of Crete's destinations. Once a small fishing village on the north-east coast of the island, Elounda is now a haven of numerous luxury hotels. Development has been both intelligent and sympathetic, allowing the natural landscape – sapphire waters, soft sandy beaches – to maintain centre-stage. Among the most exclusive resorts is Elounda Bay Palace, which surely boasts one of the most eye-catching, infinity pools imaginable. There is a main hotel building set among the jasmine – scented gardens, as well as a clutch of villas with private pools. For those who want more than a marble bathroom replete with their own Jacuzzi, then consider the two-bedroom Palace Suite or the new three-bedroom penthouse for weepingly good views over Mirabello Bay. Cocktails on the beach, fish for dinner drawn straight from the sea, tennis coursts, waterports, and two sandy beaches – you get the picture; this is the luxury lifestyle bottled for those in search of a relaxed Mediterranean getaway.

Q INSIDER: With two sandy beaches, an outdoor seawater pool, an indoor heated freshwater pool, children's paddle pool and a patient, smiling Cretan staff, Elounda Bay Palace Hotel attracts families without letting their happy cries and laughter get in the way of couples looking for some kid-free peace and quiet.

For booking enquiries contact Quintessentially Travel
Email: reserve@quintessentiallytravel.com, Tel: +44 (0)845 224 6915

GRAN MELIA RESORT & LUXURY VILLAS

CRETE, GREECE. COORDINATES – N 35° 08.865, E 025° 43.209

Gran Melia Resort & Luxury Villas Daios Cove is a hotel true to the era. Located on the north east Cretan coast, it combines traditional, local architectural forms with avant-garde design in a private bay – and all on a scale that gives guests the space they need however high their expectations. This means families or couples can enjoy a true holiday (Q particularly likes the idea of the adult-only pool, for instance, with its buzzy little wet bar; the kids, meanwhile, won't be out of their dedicated games room). There are 300 spacious rooms, suites and villas, a private sandy beach, the SPA by Germaine de Capuccini and numerous seawater infinity pools. Dining options range from classic Greek taverna cooking (seafood, eaten at beach-side tables) to an inventive 'international food bazaar'. At night it's time to dress up for a cocktail at the Crystal Box before enjoying a food-in-the-sand feast of lobster drawn from local waters.

Q INSIDER: Guests seeking more than the usual share of love and attention are well advised to step up to Red Level SM – a boutique-hotel-within-the-hotel. Here you not only benefit from the 'Red Level Lounge' but the dedicated services of personal butlers throughout your stay.

For booking enquiries contact Quintessentially Travel
Email: reserve@quintessentiallytravel.com. Tel: +44 (0)845 224 6915

NAFPLIA PALACE
HOTEL & VILLAS

NAFPLION, GREECE. COORDINATES – N 37° 33.961, E 022° 47.758

Nafplia Palace Hotel & Villas represents the meeting of two worlds: contemporary style (including the odd nod to Corbusier) folded within the walls of the third – century BC Akronafplia fortress on the shores of the Aegean (you can almost touch the ancient walls from your poolside lounger). This jewel of the Peloponnese, 20 minutes by chopper from Athens, comprises 48 seaview rooms and three family suites, three restaurants, a bar, spa and beauty centre. In addition there are 33 individually-designed villas – again, all with sea views and the use of a shared pool, private outdoor Jacuzzi or private heated pool. With views towards Argos, the oldest continuously inhabited town in Greece, you know you're at the heart of things, with major UNESCO sites, including Mycenae and the theatre of Epidaurus, close by. Add to that the hotel's gleaming marble, polished limestone and stainless steel interiors, and you've a great European hotspot for a long weekend from London, Paris or beyond.

Q INSIDER: Claiming to be the only hotel in Europe situated within an archaeological site, you owe it to the Greeks to come here. To be able to kick back in comfort with a hit of Nafplia Palace luxury in such a culturally rich region makes this a destination for the sybarite, not just the academic.

A'JIA HOTEL

ISTANBUL, TURKEY. COORDINATES – N 41° 06.904, E 029° 05.506

If Istanbul is buzzing right now then Hotel A'jia, a traditional Ottoman mansion on the shores of the Bosphorus, is where to enjoy the city's new spirit replete with a minimalist sheen. Formally called the Ahmet Rasi Pasha Mansion, the hotel comprises 16 rooms, nine of which have breathtaking views of the Bosphorus. This sparkling white hideaway is among the most discerning addresses in the capital: boutique-sized yet with a grand hotel's approach to service (it is run by the Doors Group, who are also behind a slew of the city's most fashionable nightclubs and restaurants). Five rooms have private balconies; three of the deluxe suites benefit from mezzanine levels. Although just 35 minutes from the airport, A'jia also has easy access to the city's historical and cultural attractions, the hotel located in the Bosphorus suburb of Kanlica. Modern amenities blend easily with the building's 19th-century elegance, and there is an exclusive restaurant located romantically on the waterfront serving Mediterranean cuisine.

Q INSIDER: Guests of A'Jia get complimentary use of the hotel's speedboat – a particularly Bond-like touch of glamour.

For booking enquiries contact Quintessentially Travel

KEMPINSKI HOTEL BARBAROS BAY BODRUM

BODRUM, TURKEY. COORDINATES – N 36° 59.520, E 027° 30.620

Bodrum has been having something of a comeback in recent years. New hotels big and small have injected a dose of chic, ensuring the region on the shores of the Aegean deserves its reputation as Turkey's St.Tropez. Kempinski Hotel Barbaros Bay is part of that trend – a resort featuring 25 suites and 148 rooms, each with its own terrace and bay-facing balcony located atop the Barbarbos Bay Cliff. From here you can see a beautiful picturesque view of the sea. At the resort, you've got it all–a 5,500sqm Six Senses Spa for quality therapies and detox programmes, as well as numerous restaurants offering cuisines ranging from Aegean to Asian. The white-sand beach is so clean it has been awarded a coveted blue flag. As ever with Kempinski, families will be grateful for the attentive, inclusive approach.

Q INSIDER: Take a break from the lounger and explore the numerous antique sites nearby including the amphitheatre in Ephesus, and the Artemis Temple. You can also take a trip on a Turkish gulet down the coast.

THE SOFA HOTEL
NISANTASI

ISTANBUL, TURKEY. COORDINATES – N 41° 03.029, E 028° 59.563

So often you can arrive in a 'design' hotel and forget which city you are in. This is not the case at The Sofa Hotel Nisantasi. Located in the middle of Istanbul's trendy Nisantasi neighbourhood, among the chi-chi shops, Art Nouveau buildings and knock – out restaurants, this minimalist-chic address has a serene atmosphere enriched by works of art. With 82 guestrooms, of which 17 are Executive Suites, you can expect to be nurtured by 24-hour room service and much more besides. Senior, Terrace and Executive Suites feature a kitchenette, making this your ideal home away from home. Enjoy international cuisine at Café Sofa, relax in Patika Bookstore – a place where you can browse a rare selection of books in a calm and peaceful environment – or get pampered at the SANITAS SPA (replete with Turkish bath, detox, anti-aging and thalassotherapy treatments) after a day's exploration of this bubbling metropolis. To make navigation even easier, the Osmanbey metro station is only five minutes away.

Q INSIDER: Why not enjoy a romantic getaway at The Sofa Hotel Nisantasi with a two-night stay in a Senior Suite? Enjoy a couple's massage, daily breakfast buffet, a three-course dinner and late checkout.

For booking enquiries contact Quintessentially Travel
Email: reserve@quintessentiallytravel.com, Tel: +44 (0)845 224 6915

MUSEUM HOTEL

CAPPADOCIA, TURKEY. COORDINATES – N 38° 37.997, E 34° 48.403

Cappadocia in Turkey's Anatolia is loaded with history. Numerous cultures have made roots in this curious land of valleys, canyons and sculpted rocks. Persians, Byzantines, the Seljuk Turks, Hittites, Phrygians, Greeks and Armenians – the roll-call is more exotic than any Brazilian girlfriend. Their legacy is the otherworldly vista of churches, with homes and temples carved into the sun-bleached landscape. To embrace this soul-stirring region, stay at the Museum Hotel located atop a pinnacle. More than a boutique hideaway, it consists of eight deluxe rooms and a further 22 suites, all decorated with valuable artifacts. The restaurant, Lil'a, specialises in Cappadocian and modern Turkish cuisine. Take it from Q: Cappadocia's unique sense of serenity (and the hotel's outdoor Roman pool) provide one of the best ways available to cool down from the heat of London's trading floors.

Q INSIDER: Via the hotel, pre-book a guide to explore the Goreme, Red, Ortahisar and Avanos Valleys (highlights include the Goreme Open Air Museum). Alternatively, book an early morning balloon ride and take it in from the skies.

RODINA
GRAND HOTEL & SPA

SOCHI, RUSSIA. COORDINATES – N 43° 36.015, E 039° 42.849

Rodina Grand Hotel & Spa is located in Sochi's historical centre – a city regarded as the Côte d'Azur of the Russian Riviera. At the beginning of the 19th century Russia's richest people built their country houses here, neighboring the estate of the tsarist Romanovs. In summer season it was a place of high social activity, which was followed in Soviet times by becoming the party elite's most popular vacation spot. Today Sochi attracts the celebrities of modern Russian society, so while the politics come and go, the luxury traditions remain unchanged. The 40-room hotel sits at the heart of the Sochi story, located amid a magnificent 15-hectare subtropical garden (every room has a terrace with views either of this greenery or the sea). Restaurants include day-time 'Moskva', night-time 'Black Magnolia' and 'Black Sea Beach Club', which is located on the nearby pebble beach and is supposed to be one of Sochi's best.

Q INSIDER: Rodina's hi-tech spa complex, with a total area of more than 4,000 square metres, is one of the biggest in Europe. In addition there are treatments here you find nowhere else on earth, including restorative and cosmetic programs much loved by the Russian elite.

ARARAT PARK
HYATT MOSCOW

MOSCOW, RUSSIA. COORDINATES – N 55° 45.601, E 37° 37.279

The Ararat Park Hyatt Moscow offers a welcome breath of five-star service in a city that frankly struggles with customer relations. The location is excellent, close to Red Square and a two-minute walk from Vogue Café, which is a short totter from Moscow's glamorous shops on Tverskaya Street. The hotel consists of 11 floors featuring 216 rooms and suites built around a glass-roofed, atrium-style core. The rooms have a sleek, neutral, contemporary aesthetic in warm woods, creams and browns (the six Winter Garden suites, two of which are positioned on the building's corners, have floor-to-ceiling windows that soak up all the light). Square footage is generous. There is an indoor pool, gym and spa, an Armenian restaurant, the Conservatory Lounge & Bar and a sushi bar in the lobby.

Q INSIDER: The Conservatory Lounge & Bar, located on the hotel's 10th floor, buzzes from 6pm onwards with well-known Moscow faces. In summer, from May to September, the bar spills out onto an elegant outdoor setting above the rooftops of Moscow with Bolshoi and Kremlin views.

SONORA RESORT

BRITISH COLUMBIA, CANADA. COORDINATES – N 50° 19.667, W 125° 14.961

With the Canadian spring, Sonora Resort opens its doors, from May 1st to October 15th each year. Nestled in the breathtaking Discovery Islands a 50-minute chopper ride from Vancouver International Airport, this wilderness paradise is all about huge ocean vistas and cathedral-like rainforests, where you can capture a grizzly in the lens of your camera and see whales break water right in front of you. Eagles wheel and dive and sea lions bask in the sun. Nature is close and exciting, yet there is nothing uncomfortable. Guests are cosseted by Relais & Chateaux levels of luxury and polished service as well as the exceptional cuisine for which this group is known. There is a spa for a hot-stone massage, a roof-top hot tub under the stars, the Great Hall living room for kicking back with a cocktail and numerous cosy spaces to just take in the luxury of space and nature unadulterated.

Q INSIDER: Sea Lion Pointe, a private villa, boasts an extensive collection of British Columbian artwork, breathtaking architecture, and an inviting private dining room with floor-to-ceiling windows.

For booking enquiries contact Quintessentially Travel
Email: reserve@quintessentiallytravel.com, Tel: +44 (0)845 224 6915

FAIRMONT PACIFIC RIM

VANCOUVER, CANADA. COORDINATES – N 49° 17.296, W 123° 06.987

With unobstructed views of the harbour and mountains and literally seconds away from the cruise ship terminal, the Fairmont Pacific Rim in Vancouver brings a breath of fresh air to an area rich in history and culture. Lying at the heart of the historic port and financial district, the stunning backdrop of the North Shore Mountains, Stanley Park and Coal Harbour offer unrivalled views. Sophisticated and cosmopolitan, welcoming and contemporary; the hotel combines the best of Asia and the west coast in its layout, decor and culinary offerings. Food lovers can delight in ORU – an authentic Pan-Asian bistro; Giovane – an Italian-inspired deli and cafe, and the Lobby Lounge with fabulous live entertainment six nights a week. This five-star luxury oasis with its 377 rooms is lavishly appointed with naturally-inspired materials, comfortable furnishings and state-of-the-art technology. Looking to relax? Enjoy the Willow Stream spa, full fitness centre, outdoor terrace with Jacuzzis and meditation pods with its wonderful rooftop pool and private cabanas and fire pits.

Q INSIDER: Lovers of the great outdoors are in for a treat with access to golf, ski slopes and sailing boats all in the same day. Shopping addicts and culture vultures are equally well served with a plethora of superb boutiques and world-class theatre performances just a stone's throw away.

For booking enquiries contact Quintessentially Travel
Email: reserve@quintessentiallytravel.com, Tel: +44 (0)845 224 6915

TH█GREENWICH HOTEL

NEW YORK, UNITED STATES OF AMERICA. COORDINATES – N 40° 43.194, W 074° 00.592

Located in the heart of TriBeCa, The Greenwich is a small luxury hotel of 88 rooms, all of which are different and steeped in old-world charm. How this has been achieved has much to do with the owner Robert de Niro, who clearly gets the vibe of this cinematic part of downtown Manhattan. The interior is richly layered with crafted textures, from leather armchairs to the 250 year-old Japanese house that dominates the subterranean Shibui Spa. Rooms and suites are packed with knowing collections of books in addition to well stocked and largely complimentary mini-bars. The bathrooms are either Moroccan tile or Mosaic Carrera marble, while a number of the 13 suites feature working fireplaces. More residence than hotel, the staff don't wear uniforms but are relaxed, easy and super-efficient.

Q INSIDER: If you want to splurge, book one of the two glass-roofed duplex suites on the hotel's top floor. Conceived as artists' ateliers, both feature soaring 30ft skylights, chef's kitchens, two master bedrooms, stone fireplaces and offices with separate entrances.

THE STANDARD, NEW YORK

NEW YORK, UNITED STATES OF AMERICA
COORDINATES – N 40° 44.429, W 074° 00.476

America's fourth Standard Hotel (there are two in LA and one in Miami) is in Manhattan's thriving Meatpacking District. With 337 rooms on 18 floors, The Standard, New York boasts full business amenities, extensive event space, and each room has unparalleled views of the Hudson River and the New York City skyline. Reasonably priced yet almost impossibly modish, the hotel is built above the High Line, the former elevated railroad that has been developed into New York's new favourite public park. The hotel is home to The Standard Grill, the hotel's acclaimed restaurant, The Standard Biergarten serving traditional German food and beerr, and the 18th-floor cocktail lounge that boasts 360-degree views of the city.

Q INSIDER: Check out those prices. For an Andre Balazs hotel in one of the hottest neighbourhoods in Manhattan, the bottom-rung doubles offer about as much bang for your buck as you could hope for (note that rooms looking north have spectacular views of the Empire State Building).

For booking enquiries contact Quintessentially Travel
Email: reserve@quintessentiallytravel.com, Tel: +44 (0)845 224 6915

THE MARK

NEW YORK, UNITED STATES OF AMERICA
COORDINATES – N 40° 46.521, W 073° 57.792

The Mark is housed, as it has always been, in the beautiful 1927 landmark building at the corner of 77th Street and Madison Avenue. But inside, The Mark has been completely re-imagined and given new life and identity for the 21st century. This combination of old-world comfort, avant-garde interiors and up-to-the-minute technologies makes it unique in New York, not least because of the talents of designer Jacques Grange and the hotel maestro James Sherwin. The graphic lobby is colourful and convivial, studded with unique objets d'art that surprise and intrigue. The guest rooms and suites are private havens of understated luxury. Situated on one of the Upper East Side's best blocks, surrounded by New York's premier museums, shops and restaurants, and the splendour of Central Park, The Mark not only surrounds you in luxury and style but places you at the epicentre of Manhattan's social and cultural riches.

Q INSIDER: The Mark boasts The Mark Restaurant and Mark Bar by Jean-Georges and the Frederic Fekkai Salon at The Mark (Fekkai is among the most celebrated names in hairstyling in a city where good blow-outs count for as much as Louboutins).

For booking enquiries contact Quintessentially Travel
Email: reserve@quintessentiallytravel.com, Tel: +44 (0)845 224 6915°

THE PLAZA HOTEL

NEW YORK, UNITED STATES OF AMERICA. COORDINATES – N 40° 45.859, W 073° 58.445

If you haven't already stayed, The Plaza Hotel is one of those New York fixtures that should move up your lis
pretty sharpish. In fact, it's the only New York City hotel designated as a National Historic Landmark, which is
only right with that location – at the crossroads of Fifth Avenue and Central Park South. With 282 rooms, The
Plaza has the largest overall square footage of guest rooms and suites of any luxury hotel in Manhattan. Combining
timeless tradition with a new, contemporary spirit, you can expect a panoply of five-star amenities: The Palm
Court, The Champagne Bar, The Rose Club for cocktails, a Caudalie Vinothérapie® Spa, The Shops at The Plaza
and some 21,000 square feet of event space. The Oak Room and The Oak Bar, originally opened in 1945, remain
quintessential New York experiences for both hotel guests and non-residents.

Q INSIDER: The 4,400 sq ft three-bedroom Royal Plaza Suite offers an exquisitely designed great room replete with
a grand piano and dining room, the views encompassing Fifth Avenue and Grand Army Plaza

SANCTUARY
CAMELBACK MOUNTAIN
RESORT & SPA

ARIZONA, UNITED STATES OF AMERICA
COORDINATES – N 33° 31.351, W 111° 57.581

Sanctuary Camelback Mountain Resort & Spa in Arizona seems to have it all. It is nestled atop Camelback Mountain above Scottsdale – 53 acres (and Arizona's largest infinity-edge pool) combining a tranquil, Asian-inspired spa and award-winning dining featuring farm-fresh American cuisine with Asian accents. Yet you're an easy drive from Scottsdale's shops, culture and championship golf. Guests can also enjoy hiking and biking with heart-racing views of Camelback Mountain and the surrounding desert. The contemporary-styled architecture is carried through the entire property. But it has a warmth to the aesthetic, over half the casitas offering 200 square feet of living space. Details include fireplaces, private outdoor soaking tubs, wood-block flooring and travertine marble showers. Note the property was named "#1 U.S. Resort" by Condé Nast Traveller Readers' Choice Awards in 2006.

Q INSIDER: For families or friends who want to spread out in grandeur, the Mountainside Estates at Sanctuary offer intriguing features like secluded pools, hot tubs and private patios – just a few steps away from all the resort services.

For booking enquiries contact Quintessentially Travel
Email: reserve@quintessentiallytravel.com, Tel: +44 (0)845 224 6915

CHATEAU MARMONT

LOS ANGELES, UNITED STATE OF AMERICA
COORDINATES – N 34° 05.893, W 118° 22.113

Modelled after a Loire Valley castle, Chateau Marmont is a cultural monument in its own right; this hotel's history is Hollywood. All the big names have passed through, pursued affairs in the famous suites, and escaped the paparazzi. Yet the hotel is only minutes from Beverly Hills, Hollywood and downtown LA. First opened in 1929, Chateau Marmont was acquired by Andre Balazs in 1990 who quickly added his touch of polish to the hotel's Hollywood Golden Era interiors. The eclectic suites, cottages and bungalows are set amidst lush private gardens, with the architecturally significant hillside bungalows by Craig Elwood reflecting the height of mid-century modern chic. The pool is an institution, and the bar possibly the most important watering hole in Los Angeles. Just don't forget the world-class service. As Harry Cohn, founder of Columbia Pictures, said in 1939, "If you must get in trouble, do it at the Chateau Marmont." You get the picture. This is a place you can be as public or private as you wish, staff possessing an innate understanding of the clientele's uniquely discriminating needs.

Q INSIDER: For one of the best views of Hollywood, book the two-bedroom Penthouse Suite with its 1500sq ft private terrace. Costing from $5,500 per night, Q wonders why this perfect bolthole shouldn't command more? Ergo: book early for Oscars night.

For booking enquiries contact Quintessentially Travel
Email: reserve@quintessentiallytravel.com, Tel: +44 (0)845 224 6915

AMANGIRI

UTAH, UNITED STATES OF AMERICA
COORDINATES – N 37° 00.868, W 111° 36.664

Amangiri (meaning 'peaceful mountain') is located where Utah, Colorado, New Mexico and Arizona meet. Home for centuries to the native Navajo and Hopi tribes, the region is sparsely populated, made up of deep canyons and towering plateaus. The resort's 600 acres lie within a protected valley with sweeping views over stratified rock towards the Grand Staircase in Escalante National Monument (so there's plenty to do, from ballooning to horseriding) with easy access to Grand Canyon. The architecture – as sleek as anything the Aman group is known for – centres upon a main Pavilion built around a pool. Within the Pavilion is the Living Room, Gallery (for shopping), Library, Dining Room, Private Dining Room and Cellar. Two accommodation wings lead from the Pavilion into the desert – each featuring 16 to 18 suites, all of them air-conditioned for summer with underfloor heating for the cooler months – as well as a 25,000sq ft spa offering treatments based on the ancient healing traditions of the Navajo.

Q INSIDER: The pool suites include a plunge pool, large daybed in the arrival courtyard and a private sky terrace (ideal for star gazing). And there's more: no resort in the world has a main pool like this one, constructed around a 170million-year-old rock escarpment.

For booking enquiries contact Quintessentially Travel
Email: reserve@quintessentiallytravel.com, Tel: +44 (0)845 224 6915

BLANTYRE

MASSACHUSETTS, UNITED STATES OF AMERICA
COORDINATES – N 42° 20.179, W 073° 15.545

It is easy to forget what lies outside Manhattan, but let Blantyre be a lesson to you. This beautiful, romantic country house hotel, located halfway between Boston and New York City, sits centre-stage in one of America's most culturally interesting regions. Tanglewood, summer of home of the Boston Symphony, is under three miles away. Edith Wharton's home, The Mount, is a short drive. The Norman Rockwell Museum takes under 10 minutes, and there's much more besides. Blantyre is set among 115 acres of lawn and woodlands, this lovely hotel comprised of a 1902 Tudor-style Main House with eight guestrooms, a Carriage House with 10 guestrooms and four Cottages. The style throughout recalls a gentler time of elegance and romance. Blantyre features a relaxing spa, an award-winning restaurant and an attentive, friendly staff to anticipate your every need.

Q INSIDER: While the Tanglewood season keeps the summer busy, winter turns Blantyre into a wonderland for ice-skating, snowshoeing and sleigh riding. The intimate size of the property also means Blantyre is well suited to being taken over in its entirety for family reunions and weddings.

For booking enquiries contact Quintessentially Travel
Email: reserve@quintessentiallytravel.com, Tel: +44 (0)845 224 6915

FIFTEEN BEACON HOTEL

MASSACHUSETTS, UNITED STATES OF AMERICA
COORDINATES – N 42° 21.494, W 071° 03.709

Amidst the bustle of Boston you can still find historic neighbourhoods featuring quaint brick sidewalks and authentic Federal and Greek Revival row houses. This is where you also find Fifteen Beacon. A luxury boutique hotel in a Beaux Arts building, this 62-room haven is immensely comfortable, uncluttered and equipped with state-of-the-art technology: gas fireplaces, iHome alarm clock radios, surround-sound stereos, cordless phones, complimentary wireless Internet access and 42-inch flat screen televisions. With seven guest rooms per floor, guests experience the intimacy of a private residence combined with highly personal service. Each room, in taupe, cream and espresso, is balanced with modern and antique furniture that conspire to give the hotel its traditional New England soul. Mooo is the hotel's culinary twist on the traditional steakhouse – open for breakfast, brunch, lunch and dinner (there is also an all-day bar menu).

Q INSIDER: A Lexus house car provides a complimentary drop-off service anywhere in Boston; for airport transfers, the Lexus costs a very reasonable one-way $40.

For booking enquiries contact Quintessentially Travel
Email: reserve@quintessentiallytravel.com, Tel: +44 (0)845 224 6915

WYNN
LAS VEGAS & ENCORE

LAS VEGAS, UNITED STATES OF AMERICA
COORDINATES – N 36° 07.582, W 115° 09.956

Wynn Las Vegas and Encore comprise some 5,000 rooms and suites. Guests are spoi[l]
for choice when it comes to leisure activities. There are 21 mouth watering restaurants
an array of designer boutiques, two full-service spas and salons, as well sizzling pool
and incredible shows to enjoy (including Le Rêve, an aquatic spectacle). As if thi[s]
was not enough, there is an18-hole golf course designed by world-renowned architec[t]
Tom Fazio and ultra chic nightclubs and lounges. For Q, however, there's no nee[d]
to be intimidated by the numbers; there's only one thing you need to really know
about—the Tower Suites, attended by a team of VIP concierges and offering a privat[e]
entrance, dedicated registration lounge and exclusive pool access.

Q INSIDER: Pack every credit card you have. The repertoire of retailers at the Wyn[n]
and Encore Esplanades includes Manolo Blahnik, Brioni, Cartier, Chanel, Oscar de l[a]
Renta, Dior, Graff, Hermès, Alexander McQueen, Rock & Republic and Louis Vuitto[n]

For booking enquiries contact Quintessentially Travel
Email: reserve@quintessentiallytravel.com, Tel: +44 (0)845 224 6915

THE SETAI

FLORIDA, UNITED STATES OF AMERICA
COORDINATES – N 25° 47.753, W 080° 07.719

The Setai is among Miami's latest scene-stealers with its white sand beach, three pools, 85 guestrooms, 45 suites, an Asian-inspired spa and restaurants. Even the in-room amenities come courtesy of Asprey (A-lister or otherwise, they know you will be slipping these goodies in your bag on departure). The Setai is a very private place that makes you feel serene whatever the stresses of your life. The gardens are an oasis of tropical colour and the service protective. The suites are so well designed they compete with guests' private homes – we are talking all the big players in music, fashion and film – combining black granite and teak with crisp whites. But then The Setai is the summation of a powerful vision, that of Adrian Zecha, the Singaporean founder of Amanresorts.

Q INSIDER: The 10,000sq ft Penthouse features a rooftop pool and sweeping panoramas of the ocean, beach and Miami skyline. Book it for a money-no-object vacation. Alternatively, it's the SoBe venue par excellence for a private reception.

For booking enquiries contact Quintessentially Travel
Email: reserve@quintessentiallytravel.com, Tel: +44 (0)845 224 6915

DELANO

FLORIDA, UNITED STATES OF AMERICA
COORDINATES – N 25° 47.528, W 080° 07.770

Located in the heart of South Beach and directly on the ocean, Delano almost invented the concept of the 'urban resort hotel'. In a completely original manipulation of space, Delano boasts the first 'indoor/outdoor' lobby, offering a seamless flow between a series of environments; this means the sunshine that defines Miami Beach year-round soaks into the building and its 194 rooms. Philippe Starck has assembled a stunning international collection of furniture and objects, including works from such renowned artists as Antonio Gaudi, Man Ray, Charles and Ray Eames, Salvador Dali and Mark Newson. It is this kind of thinking detail that makes a stay memorable – with no oversights to speak of. Even the pool features underwater music.

Q INSIDER: Miami Beach – or more specifically, Delano – is all about kicking back beneath the beaming sunshine, cocktail in hand and listening to a DJ while revelling in the fact you are here, right here, beside one of the hippest pools on the planet. Don't rush your stay here, but instead book in for a very, very long weekend.

For booking enquiries contact Quintessentially Travel
Email: reserve@quintessentiallytravel.com, Tel: +44 (0)845 224 6915

MONDRIAN

FLORIDA, UNITED STATES OF AMERICA
COORDINATES – N 25° 46.918, W 080° 08.560

Located on newly fashionable West Avenue, Mondrian is a quiet enclave minutes from the bustling centre of South Beach, offering spectacular views of the Atlantic Ocean, Biscayne Bay and downtown Miami. The visionary style of designer Marcel Wanders is apparent from the moment you pull into the porte-cochere: guests walk through a grand entryway appointed with custom-designed furniture, lighting and accent pieces (Wanders' calls it 'Sleeping Beauty's Castle'). The floor-to-ceiling windows offer stunning views of Biscayne Bay. Immediately the eye is drawn to the masterpiece of the room – an iconic 'floating' staircase. Lush gardens hung with hammocks and a stunning pool (there's a separate kids' pool and large cabanas available for family rental) are just the beginning of this quintessential Miami Beach story, rooms and suites providing serene retreats from the Mondrian's buzz and hubbub.

Q INSIDER: Out on the bay you can enjoy activities such as jet skis, boating and watersports.

For booking enquiries contact Quintessentially Travel
Email: reserve@quintessentiallytravel.com, Tel: +44 (0)845 224 6915

LAS VENTANAS AL PARAÍSO, A ROSEWOOD RESORT

BAJA CALIFORNIA SUR, MEXICO
COORDINATES – N 22° 58.636, W 109° 46.168

Las Ventanas al Paraíso, A Rosewood Resort is dramatically located on a pristine white-sand beach along the Sea of Cortez on Pacific Coast Mexico. It is backed by a starkly beautiful desert landscape; in front lies one of the world's richest marine environments offering world-class sport fishing, snorkeling, scuba diving, yachting, sea kayaking, surfing and windsurfing. When it first opened in 1997, Las Ventanas immediately became the standard by which all other luxury hotels in the neighbourhood would be measured. Thirteen years on and it still wields a giant reputation. Yet there are only 71 suites, all with butler service. Cuisine includes Baja-Mediterranean dishes served in The Restaurant, and the Sea Grill's Cocina del Fuego where the freshest possible fish is cooked on wood-burning grills. The resort's Tequila & Ceviche Bar is known for its list of tequilas, becoming a Tequila & Sushi Bar in the evening.

Q INSIDER: The golfer has four spectacular public courses to choose from including the 18-hole Robert Trent Jones II Cabo Real course that wraps around Las Ventanas. You can also go whale-watching. Or do as Q recommends, and hole up for days in the exceptional Las Ventanas spa.

For booking enquiries contact Quintessentially Travel
Email: reserve@quintessentiallytravel.com, Tel: +44 (0)845 224 6915

NANDANA

WEST END, GRAND BAHAMA. COORDINATES – N 26° 40.252 W 078° 57.813

Nandana is something new for Grand Bahama: an Asian beach-house style residence built by a world-class architect. With more than 18,000 square feet of interior living space, this gated oceanfront estate has all the bells and whistles Q has come to expect from a part of the world where standards are high and rising all the time. There's Nandana's world-class cuisine, a heated 120ft infinity pool, Jacuzzi, fully equipped gym, in-house spa, library, 400-bottle wine cellar and private office with global connectivity, all supported by an experienced, professionally trained hotel staff. There is even a boat captain at your beck and call. The thing we didn't tell you is how few Nandana sleeps: 10 guests. In other words, you've got the polish of a hotel while revelling in the discretion and square footage offered by a vast private home.

Q INSIDER: A 43ft yacht is available to guests for deep-sea, bone fishing and scuba diving excursions. The property also offers a fleet of Yamaha wave runners, a Land Rover Defender, Suzuki All-Terrain vehicles and golf carts as well as private landing facility. Note a brand-new golf course designed by pro-golfer Jack Nicklaus is located two minutes away from Nandana.

For booking enquiries contact Quintessentially Travel
Email: reserve@quintessentiallytravel.com, Tel: +44 (0)845 224 6915

NECKER ISLAND

VIRGIN GORDA, BRITISH VIRGIN ISLANDS
COORDINATES – N 18° 31.443, W 64° 21.516

It is no secret who owns this rather impressive private island: Sir Richard Branson. Located in the British Virgin Islands, Necker comprises 74 acres encircled by coral reefs and white beaches making it the tropical escape perfected. Between The Great House and five Balinese-style villas, Necker sleeps 28. You can take it on an exclusive basis, or room by room during specific weeks – a flexibility that's rare among private islands). Eat what you like, where you like, when you like. Necker comes with great chefs (for anything from lobster to a traditional English roast) as well as a stunning wine cellar. A team of 50 staff are on hand, including massage therapists. Think of it as your own private resort with a spa and every possible watersport available with a nod of your head.

Q INSIDER: Live out your James Bond fantasies with the Necker Nymph, a three-person aero submarine berthed at Necker Island that can dive down to a depth of 30 metres. With a trained pilot at the helm, explore ancient shipwrecks and exotic marine life. Note you need at least a PADI open water dive certificate to come on board.

For booking enquiries contact Quintessentially Travel
Email: reserve@quintessentiallytravel.com, Tel: +44 (0)845 224 6915

EDEN ROCK – ST. BARTHS

ST. BARTHÉLEMY, FRENCH WEST INDIES
COORDINATES – N 17° 54.195, W 062° 50.169

Eden Rock in St.Barths is a legend that evolved from an imaginatively sited private house built about 60 years ago by Rémy de Haenen – a pioneering aviator and treasure seeker who became the first Mayor of the Island of St.Barths. His pleasure-loving spirit lives on. Under the ownership of the Matthews family since 1995, the original house has been lovingly restored with the addition of new villas. A more dreamy place is hard to imagine, for the hotel is located on a rocky promontory surrounded by white coral, sandy beaches and a coral reef in St. Jean Bay. Impeccable attention to detail and service ensures regulars – artists, musicians, world-famous gourmands – are quick to rebook for the following year. Those who can't wrangle a suite can instead be found brunching for hours over the fresh Breton oysters at the foot-in-the-sand restaurant on the beach.

Q INSIDER: Of the 34 superbly different accommodations, there are two that stand out: Villa Nina, with its own art gallery, and Villa Rockstar with a music recording studio and one bathroom tiled of pure white gold.

For booking enquiries contact Quintessentially Travel
Email: reserve@quintessentiallytravel.com, Tel: +44 (0)845 224 6915

HOTEL ST BARTH ISLE DE FRANCE

ST. BARTHÉLEMY, FRENCH WEST INDIES
COORDINATES – N 17° 55.156, W 062° 51.294

Hotel St Barth Isle de France is positioned on arguably the best beach of all the resorts on this tiny Caribbean island – the blindingly white Baie des Flamands. Many rooms are ocean facing. Others are plantation-style garden cottages (some have interconnecting doubles, ideal for families). The look is fresh and cool, with whitewashed walls accented with antiques and vintage French fabrics. It is elegant, easy, effortlessly chic, which is also the tone around the pool where guests (as many as 75 per cent are regulars) emerge for a late French-style breakfast. At La Case de l'Isle restaurant, Head Chef Yann Vinsot offers up delicious local fish dishes like salmon tartare with green apples and herbs or the mouth – watering local yellow tuna caramelised with Asian flavours. For the ultimate in relaxation, there is a Molton Brown-designed spa and when the sun goes down, trendy hipsters head towards the funky Caribbean-style Beach Bar or the hotel's Sundowner Deck for elegant cocktails.

Q INSIDER: As of December 2010, there are two three-bedroom Flamands Villas available, perfect for those seeking exclusivity, luxury and privacy. Situated on the flawless Baie des Flamands, guests can enjoy their own living room, fitness rooms, home cinema and the most state-of-the-art amenities making for a veritable heaven on earth.

For booking enquiries contact Quintessentially Travel
Email: reserve@quintessentiallytravel.com, Tel: +44 (0)845 224 6915

PARROT CAY

PROVIDENCIALES, TURKS AND CAICOS ISLANDS
COORDINATES – N 21° 56.075, W 072° 03.164

Parrot Cay in the Turks and Caicos is a powerful example of the luxury o
simplicity. Nature is celebrated, the mile-long, 1000-acre island ringed i
porcelain-white sand, pristine diving reefs and deep turquoise sea. Bird lif
is rich, with tall egrets populating moody wetlands (much of the island ha
been left deliberately undeveloped). The resort's chic aesthetic is non-invasive
consisting of airy, light-filled rooms and beachside villas with gardens, verandah
and private beach. Guests can rediscover a more relaxed rhythm at the resort'
COMO Shambhala Retreat, an award-winning spa offering sophisticate
therapies from Ayurveda to acupuncture. The resort also hosts specific Retrea
Weeks led by top teachers such as American Yoga master Rodney Yee, this is i
addition to Pilates sesssions and a regular program of complimentary activities
Cuisine ranges from Mediterranean to Asian and Caribbean as well as healthfu
options, with meals enjoyed poolside or in the Terrace Restaurant.

Q INSIDE: Parrot Cay Estate is a collection of beachside homes for traveller
who seek the ultimate villa experience with hotel services attached. No-on
will bother you on the concealed stretch of beach, the properties located a fiv
to 10 minute buggy ride from the main resort.

For booking enquiries contact Quintessentially Travel
Email: reserve@quintessentiallytravel.com, Tel: +44 (0)845 224 6915

VICEROY ANGUILLA

BARNES BAY, ANGUILLA. COORDINATES – N 18° 10.865, W 063° 08.251

Set in the British West Indies and surrounded by the Eastern Caribbean, Anguilla is revered for its pristine soft white sand beaches – 33 altogether – and crystal clear turquoise waters. Situated on 35 lush acres, with 3,200 feet of beachfront land along the white sands of Barnes and Meads Bays, Viceroy Anguilla adds to the island's attractions: a super-cool, glamorous Caribbean address where the likes of Samuel L Jackson and Orlando Bloom have already put a toe or two in the water. The 166 contemporary accommodations including a number of sophisticated townhomes, opulent resort residences and 31 four or five-bedroom beachfront and bluff – top villas. Interiors are by hotshot designer Kelly Wearstler who has created a strong sense of the island in driftwood lamps, and petrified – wood tables combined with travertine marble floors, hand-carved wood pieces from Asia, hammered metalwork from India and beaded artwork from Africa. There are five restaurants, as well as a new nutrition-focused wellness menu launching this year.

Q INSIDER: The 8,000sq ft spa offers a myriad of wellness rituals including massages, body polishes, wraps, facials, mani-pedicures, a sea mist infinity pool, three outdoor treatment cabanas and high-tech Vichy shower for specialised hydrotherapy treatments.

PONTA DOS GANCHOS EXCLUSIVE RESORT

SANTA CATARINA, BRAZIL. COORDINATES – S 27° 18.313, W 048° 33.057

Ponta dos Ganchos is a rare Brazilian member of Relais & Chateaux. Situated on a small point nestling between two simple fishing villages, and surrounded on three sides by the sea of the Emerald Coast, it is a 50-minute drive from Florianopolis Airport, which in its turn is a one-hour flight from São Paulo. The Governador Celso Ramos region, a slice of old Brazil, is sparsely populated with descendents of the original Azorean settlers. There are only 25 comfortable and spacious 'bungalows', all with sea views, in an area of over 80,000 square metres. With over three staff per bungalow, the resort offers highly customised service (breakfast, lunch and dinner available at any hour). The style is rustic-chic, but the facilities comprehensive: air conditioning, 32" LCD televisions with local and satellite channels, WiFi Internet connections, wine cellars and fireplaces.

Q INSIDER: The Restaurant, which is metres from the beach, is one of the reasons why many people come, the Brazilian cuisine well known to the great and good of South America. For a private assignation, book 'Dinner on the Island', decorated at night with flowers and candles.

For booking enquiries contact Quintessentially Travel
Email: reserve@quintessentiallytravel.com, Tel: +44 (0)845 224 6915

H TEL UNIQUE

SÃO PAULO, BRAZIL. COORDINATES – S 23° 34.912 W 046° 40.010

Hotel Unique is exactly that – a five-star hotel that goes beyond the usual reference points of a top-class address. This has much to do with the vision of Brazilian architect Ruy Ohtake who created a huge inverted arc – 100m long by 25m tall – faced with 1.8m-diameter circular windows. The curvaceous design means all 95 suites and apartments benefit from the rich Brazilian sunshine, with views overlooking Ibirapuera Park or the tree-lined, upscale Jardins neighbourhood of which this hotel is such an important part. Interior decor is by fellow Brazilian João Armentano. In a city obsessed by how things look, Armentano has pulled off something impressive; he has managed to deliver function (running mineral water through the taps and showers, automatic blackout curtains...), not just a beautiful form (the scarlet swimming pool being the hotel's knock – out feature).

Q INSIDER: While Q loves the havaianas provided in-room to every guest on arr   (staff assume you will steal these too-cool-for-school Brazilian flip-flops), Paulistas will tell you it is the penthouse Skye restaurant which has the city talking with global gourmet menus conceived by Emmanuel Bassoleil.

For booking enquiries contact Quintessentially Travel
Email: reserve@quintessentiallytravel.com, Tel: +44 (0)845 224 6915

HOTEL FASANO
SÃO PAULO

SÃO PAULO, BRAZIL. COORDINATES – S 23° 33.884, W 046° 40.163

For over a century, the Fasano family has created some of the best gourmet dining environments São Paulo has to offer. It brings this talent to the management of the most charming hotel in the city, the Fasano, where designers Isay Weinfeld and Márcio Kogan have crafted a distinctly elegant 1930's throwback-style ambience. Such work can be seen in the façade bricks, imported from England, and the lobby marble beams from Rome. A dedicated butler team delivers polished, non-invasive service. The award-winning Italian restaurant is one of the hottest addresses in town even eight years on from opening. The other perennial favourite is the jazz bar, Baretto, where Brazil's opinion makers, glamour pusses and captains of industry mingle with an international jet-set.

Q INSIDER: The hotel is located between the business centres of Paulista and Faria Lima, with the likes of Dior, Vuitton and Tiffanys in dangerously close striking distance.

For booking enquiries contact Quintessentially Travel
Email: reserve@quintessentiallytravel.com, Tel: +44 (0)845 224 6915

HOTEL FASANO
RIO DE JANEIRO

RIO DE JANEIRO, BRAZIL. COORDINATES – S 22° 59.230, W 043° 11.769

Located in the heart of Ipanema Beach, Hotel Fasano Rio de Janeiro combines the sophistication of Rio's most coveted address with modernity and efficiency in design and service. Envisioned by Philippe Starck, everything has been thought out to reflect the glorious 'bossa nova' era. Guests can experience the Fasano family's long-standing gastronomic reputation at the elegant Fasano al Mare restaurant – a Mediterranean seafood restaurant under the command of Fogerio Fasano and Luca Gozzani – or signature cocktails and light meals at the 'sceney' Baretto-Londra. The breathtaking view from the rooftop swimming pool overlooks Ipanema and Leblon beaches and the Corcovado. And then there are those rooms – the perfect retreat from all the sun and glamour.

Q INSIDER: The lobby lounge bar evokes an inviting, familiar atmosphere with antique designer furniture, books, goose-down couches and a stunning mirror-carved bar – a key hub for the city's great and good in their Havainos and three-inch heels. Here, anything goes, so long as it is the height of Rio style.

For booking enquiries contact Quintessentially Travel
Email: reserve@quintessentiallytravel.com, Tel: +44 (0)845 224 6915

POUSADA PICINGUABA

UBATUBA, BRAZIL. COORDINATES – S 23° 22.680, W 044° 50.242

Surrounded by UNESCO World-Heritage tropical forest, the Pousada Picinguaba is located half-way between Rio de Janeiro and São Paulo and just 30 minutes from the colonial town of Paraty. Overlooking the peaceful bay of Picinguaba, the Pousada is the perfect choice for a slow-paced escape in a charming fishing village. The unpretentious colonial-style house offers 10 rooms all opening onto the natural surroundings, including a honeymoon suite with breathtaking ocean views. Private villas are situated a few steps from the Pousada's entrance. For the experienced traveller looking for a romantic or family escape, relaxation, discovery, adventure, or for a small private venue, there is nothing to disturb nature's magic: no TV, Internet or air-conditioning. Experience a different world, where the only sounds are the wind in the palm trees and the sea gently lapping on the shore. Where deserted beaches and untouched rainforests are discoverable by foot, kayak or on the Pousada's schooner.

Q INSIDER: What gives the Pousada its soul is the interaction with the small village from which it takes its name. At Picinguaba you are received by real people who are born in the area. Make the most of it by getting out to explore – and by visiting Paraty, another UNESCO town a 30-minute drive away.

For booking enquiries contact Quintessentially Travel
Email: reserve@quintessentiallytravel.com, Tel: +44 (0)845 224 6915

FAENA HOTEL+UNIVERSE

BUENOS AIRES, ARGENTINA
COORDINATES – S 34° 36.843, W 058° 21.726

How do you make cutting edge design work its charm within the grandeur of the century-old historic building that houses the five-star Faena Hotel + Universe? Well, you commission the talents of Philippe Starck and Alan Faena whose creations display a renowned sense of innovation and aesthetic beauty. Their characteristic attention to detail complements the high quality natural materials on display, like lapacho wood and arabasceto marble, reminiscent of the re-birth of the sumptuous Belle Epoque. Flashes of deep red bring a touch of drama to the Imperial furniture, luxurious velvet curtains, fabrics and tall crystal mirrors that incorporate traditional Argentine themes and patterns throughout. One hundred guestrooms and a range of memorable suites look onto the Rio de la Plata – the world's widest river – or the docks and fabulous city of Buenos Aires on the other. Faena is one of the few hotels in Buenos Aires with an outdoor swimming pool. Located inside a terraced garden enjoy the warm rays of the southern hemisphere sunshine while enjoying light meals and cocktails. How the other side lives!

Q INSIDER: Wine lovers will be in seventh heaven in Faena's Wine Cellar-over 500 labels are stored within its brick walls where award-winning Chief Sommelier Aldo Graziani oversees tastings and private dinners for groups of up to 16 people.

For booking enquiries contact Quintessentially Travel
Email: reserve@quintessentiallytravel.com, Tel: +44 (0)845 224 6915

LLAO LLAO HOTEL & RESORT, GOLF – SPA

RIO NEGRO, ARGENTINA. COORDINATES – S 41° 3.437, W 71° 31.418

Llao Llao Hotel & Resort, Golf-Spa, is located in Argentine Patagonia – one of the world's most dramatic mountainscapes. The resort has been here since 1940 (the Bustillo Wing), which is reflected in the architecture: a Canadian-style building with Norman roof tiles, cypress logs and the region's green stone. It now features 170 guestrooms, 29 suites and a cabin. You can choose the cozy, classical Llao Llao style or take one of the studios and suites facing Moreno Lake and the Mount Tronador – all featuring LCD TVs, private terraces, Jacuzzis and air conditioning. Los Cesares Restaurant is for haute cuisine; Patagonia restaurant has a more relaxed ambience. There is a spa, an indoor/outdoor pool and an 18-hole golf course. Further activities include trekking, mountain biking, skiing, fishing and windsurfing as well as winter skiing at Cerro Catedral (July to September).

Q INSIDER: Llao Llao's English-speaking staff is committed to making everybody feel at home – including children. The resort's Nahuelito's Kids Club is the ideal place to have fun and connect with nature.

HOTEL DE LARACHE

SAN PEDRO DE ATACAMA, CHILE
COORDINATES – S 22° 54.982, W 068° 12.002

explora Atacama is more than an adventure hotel; it is a right of passage for anyone interested in the deep cultural history of a very ancient part of South America. The first humans arrived in this Chilean desert over 10,000 years ago, giving rise to what later became a rich culture concentrated in and around oases like the one at San Pedro where the hotel is located. It gets more interesting still, for diverse and unusual forms of wildlife have found ways to develop in the midst of the region's high volcanoes, salt flats, lagoons and ravines. All this is yours to discover by foot, bicycle, boat or horseback guided by explora's expert staff. At the end of the day, expect to be nurtured within the luxury confines of the lodge, all 46 rooms and four suites drenched in sunshine. There is also an observatory for viewing the night sky, and an area of heated pools, open-air Jacuzzis, saunas and steam baths.

Q INSIDER: explora Atacama has built eight large, interconnected pools in a spot about 45 minutes from the hotel. This is in order to take advantage of the thermal waters that spring forth from a large ravine. Some of explora's explorations end at these pools, known as the Termas de Puritama.

For booking enquiries contact Quintessentially Travel
Email: reserve@quintessentiallytravel.com, Tel: +44 (0)845 224 6915

EXPLORA PATAGONIA

PUERTO NATALES, CHILE. COORDINATES – S 51° 07.412, W 073° 07.851

Patagonia is the southernmost region of the American continent and one of the least populated areas in the world. Millions of years ago, it underwent major geological and glaciological transformations that created mountains, glaciers, lakes and rivers. Today this region is home to an extensive variety of plants and animals, many of which are native to the area. The region is also home to Hotel Salto Chico, or explora Patagonia, which is the only lodge at the centre of Torres del Paine National Park. Covering some 242,242 hectares, this vast wilderness sequesters 105 types of birds and several species of mammals, some in large numbers, others far more rare, including the puma. The hotel stands on the shores of Lake Pehoe, the building's boldly contemporary architecture maximising the extraordinary panoramic views from all 30 rooms. There is also a sauna, gym and outdoor Jacuzzis with glaciers in your very viewshed.

Q INSIDER: The lodge's experienced guides will help tailor activities to your level of fitness, from hikes to the magnificent grey glacier or to the landlocked blue lagoons. Such excursions are included in the well-priced four and eight-night programmes available year-round.

For booking enquiries contact Quintessentially Travel
Email: reserve@quintessentiallytravel.com, Tel: +44 (0)845 224 6915

INDIGO PATIGONIA

PUERTO NATALES, CHILE
COORDINATES – S 51° 43.926, W 072° 30.576

Hotel Spa Indigo Patagonia is the result of three owners – French, Chilean and Spanish – coming together in a part of the world they all fell in love with as adventurers, mountaineers, gourmands and wine aficionados. Patagonia is a place where people come looking for extreme experiences – and this hotel bottles its essence. The property is located on the sea front of Puerto Natales and looks at the Fjord of Last Hope, at glaciers Serrano and Balmaceda, and at the impressive Paine Mountains. The hotel is a one-hour drive from Torres Del Paine National Park, a wilderness guests can explore with guided activities from kayak excursions to horseback rides. Some, however, will want to do nothing but relax in the minimalist, comfortable rooms, enjoying the hotel's spa and outdoor Jacuzzis. In short, this is a place to take time out and recuperate in one of the world's most unspoiled, energy-giving regions.

Q INSIDER: The three and four-night adventure packages offer a seamless, cost-effective way of exploring Patagonia with excellent food, reliable guiding, transport, and at the end of the day, a comfortable bed. In this part of the world, that's a luxury that's rare.

For booking enquiries contact Quintessentially Travel
Email: reserve@quintessentiallytravel.com, Tel: +44 (0)845 224 6915

PROPERTY INDEX

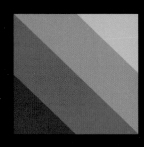

AFRICA & INDIAN OCEAN
ASIA & PACIFIC
EUROPE
THE AMERICAS

Shangri-La Villingli – Page 16
Villingli Island, Addu Atoll, Maldives
Email: info@shangri – la.com
www.shangri-la.com   Tel: +960 689 7888

Naladhu Maldives – Page 18
Veligandu Huraa, South Male Atoll, Maldives
Email: stay@naladhu.com
www.naladhu.com Tel: +960 664 1888

Cocoa Island – Page 20
Makunufushi, South Malé Atoll, Cocoa Island, Maldives
Email: res@cocoaisland.como.bz
www.cocoaisland.como.bz Tel: +960 6641818

Baros Maldives Resort & Spa – Page 22
Baros, Malé, Maldives, 2015
Email: info@baros.com
www.baros.com Tel: +960 664 26 72

Velassaru Maldives – Page 23
Velassaru Maldives, South Malé Atoll, Maldives
Email: info@velassaru.com
www.velassaru.com Tel: + 960 333 2271

Maradiva Villas Resort & Spa – Page 24
Maradiva, Wolmar, Mauritius
Email: info@maradiva.com
www.maradiva.com Tel: +230 403 1625

Shanti Maurice, a Nira Resort – Page 25
Rivière des Galets , Chemin Grenier, Maurice, Mauritius
Email: info@shantiananda.com
www.shantiananda.com Tel: +23 060 37200

Oberoi Mauritius – Page 26
Baie aux Tortues, Pointe aux Piments, Mauritius
Email: reservation.mauritius@oberoihotels.com
www.oberoihotels.com Tel: +91 – 11 – 2389 0505

Banyan Tree Seychelles – Page 27
Anse Intendance, Mahe, Republic of Seychelles
Email: seychelles@banyantree.com
www.banyantree.com Tel: +248 383 500

Raffles Praslin, Seychelles – Page 28
Anse Takamaka, Praslin, Seychelles
Email: praslin@raffles.com
www.seychellesraffles.com Tel: +248 296 000

North Island – Page 29
North Island, Victoria, Mahe, Seychelles
Email: info@north-island.com
www.north-island.com Tel: +248 293 100

Royal Mansour, Marrakech – Page 30
Rue Abou Abbas El Sebti, Marrakech, 4000, Morocco
Email: reservation@royalmansour.ma
www.royalmansour.ma Tel: +212 (0) 5 24 37 83 39

Amanjena – Page 31
Route de Ouarzazate km 12, Marrakech, Morocco
Email: amanjena@amanresorts.com
www.amanresorts.com Tel: +212 5 24 403 353

Kasbah Du Toubkal – Page 32
Kasbah Du Toubkal BP 31, Asni, Nr Marrakech, Morocco
Email: info@kasbahdutoubkal.com
www.kasbahdutoubkal.com Tel: + 33(0)5 49 05 01 35

Bilila Lodge – Page 34
Bilila Lodge Kempinski, Serengeti, Tanzania
Email: reservations.tanzania@kempinski.com
www.kempinski.com/en/serengeti Tel: +255 778 888 888

&Beyond Mnemba Island Lodge – Page 35
Mnemba Archipelago, Zanzibar
Email: res@personalafrica.com
www.mnemba-island.com Tel: +2711 463 6586

Lion Sands Private Game Reserve – Page 36
Sabi Sand Game Reserve, Mpumalanga, South Africa
Email: res@lionsands.com
www.lionsands.com Tel: +27 11 484 9911

Royal Malewane – Page 37
Kruger National Park, 1380, South Africa
Email: info@royalmalewane.com
www.royalmalewane.com Tel: +27 (0)15 793 0150

Molori Safari Lodges – Page 38
Molori Clifton, Cape Town, South Africa
Email: info@molori.com
www.molori.com

Tintswalo Atlantic – Page 39
Hout Bay, Cape Town, South Africa
Email: reception@atlantic.tintswalo.com
www.tintswalo.com Tel: +27 (0) 87 754 9300

Morukuru Lodge – Page 40
Madikwe Game Reserve, 2838, South Africa
Email: info@morukuru.com
www.morukuru.com Tel: +31 229 299 555

Cape Grace – Page 41
West Quay Road, Victoria & Alfred
Waterfront, Cape Town, South Africa
Email: info@capegrace.com
www.capegrace.com Tel: +27 21 410 7100

Emirates Palace – Page 44
West End Corniche, Abu Dhabi, UAE
Email: info.emiratespalace@kempinski.com
www.emiratespalace.com Tel: +971 2 690 9000

Burj al Arab – Page 46
Dubai, 74147, UAE
Email: BAAreservations@jumeirah.com
www.burj-al-arab.com Tel: +971 4 301 7777

Armani Hotel Dubai – Page 48
1 Emaar Boulevard, Burj Khalifa, Downtown Dubai, UAE
Email: reservations.dubai@armanihotels.com
www.armanihotels.com Tel: +971 4 888 3999

Raffles Dubai – Page 50
Sheikh Rashid Road, Wafi, Dubai, UAE
Email: dubai@raffles.com
www.raffles.com Tel: +971 4324 8888

W Doha Hotel & Residences – Page 51
West Bay, Doha, 19573, Qatar
Email: info@whotels.doha.com
 www.WHotelDoha.com Tel: +974 4453 5000

Shangri-La Barr Al Jissah Resort & Spa – Page 52
Muscat, Sultanate of Oman, 644
Email: info@shangri-la.com
www.shangri-la.com Tel: +968 2477 6666

The Chedi Muscat – Page 54
Al Khuwair, Muscat, Sultante of Oman
Email: reservation@chedimuscat.com
www.ghmhotels.com Tel: +968 24 52 44 00

Devi Garh – Page 55
Delwara NH – 8, Near Eklingji Udaipur, Gurgaon, Rajsamand
Email: devigarh@deviresorts.com
www.deviresorts.com Tel: +91 2953 289 211

Devi Ratn – Page 56
Jamdoli, Agra Road, Tehsil Ballupura, Jaipur, Rajasthan
Email: deviratn@deviresorts.com
www.deviresorts.in/deviratn Tel: +91 141 3050211

Rasa Jaipur – Page 57
Kunda – NH 8, Tehsil Amer, Rajasthan, District Jaipur
Email: rasajaipur@rasaresorts.in
www.rasaresorts.in Tel: + 91 124 4888 011/022

The Leela Palace Kempinski Udaipur – Page 58
Lake Pichola, Lake Pichola, Rajasthan, India
Email: reservations.udaipur@theleela.com
www.theleela.com Tel: +91 294670 1234

Amanbagh – Page 59
Ajabargh, Rajasthan, India
Email: amanbagh@amanresorts.com
www.amanresorts.com Tel: +91 1465 223 333

St. Regis Bangkok – Page 60
159 Rajadamri Road, Bangkok, 10330, Thailand
Email: stregis.bangkok@stregis.com
www.starwoodhotels.com Tel: +66 2207 7777

Amanpuri – Page 62
Pansea Beach , Phuket, 83000, Thailand
Email: amanpuri@amanresorts.com
www.amanresorts.com Tel: +66 76 324 333

Trisara – Page 63
60/1Moo 6, Srisoonthorn Road, Cherngtalay, Thalang, Phuket
Email: reservations@trisara.com
www.trisara.com Tel: +66 76 310100

Sri Panwa Estate – Page 64
88 Moo 8 Sakdidej Road, Tambon Vichit, Phuket,
Email: chill@sripanwa.com
www.sripanwa.com Tel: +66 76 371000

Anantara Phuket Villas – Page 65
888 Moo 3 Tumbon Mai Khao , Amphur Thalang, Phuket
Email: phuket@anantara.com
www.phuket.anantara.com Tel: +66 (0)76 336 100

Baan Taling Ngam Resort & Spa – Page 66
295 Moo 3, Taling Ngam Beach, Koh Samui, Suratthani
Email: rsvn@baan-taling-ngam.com
www.baan-taling-ngam.com Tel: +66 7742 9100

W Retreat Koh Samui – Page 67
4/1 Moo 1, T.Maenam, Koh Samui, Surat Thani
Email: w.kohsamui@whotels.com
www.whotels.com/kohsamui Tel: +66 77 915999

Pangkor Laut Resort – Page 68
Pangkor Laut Island, Lumut, Perak, Malaysia
Email: info@pangkorlautresort.com
www.pangkorlautresort.com Tel: +60 3 2783 1000

Tanjong Jara Resort – Page 69
Batu 8, Off Jalan Dungun, Dungun, Terengganu, Malaysia
Email: info@tanjongjararesort.com
www.tanjongjararesort.com Tel: +603 2783 1000

The Club at The Saujana – Page 70
Saujana Resort, Jalan Lapangan Terbang
SAAS, Shah Alam, Selangor
Email: info@thesaujana.com
www.theclubatthesaujana.com Tel: +603 7843 1234

Raffles Hotel, Singapore – Page 71
1 Beach Road, 189673, Singapore
Email: singapore@raffles.com
www.raffles.com/singapore Tel: +65 6337 1886

Fuchun Resort – Page 87
Hangfu Yanjiang Road, Hangzhou, Zheijiang
Email: reservation@fuchunresort.com
www.fuchunresort.com Tel: +86 571 6346 1111

The Fullerton Hotel – Page 72
1 Fullerton Square, 049178, Singapore
Email: info@fullertonhotel.com
www.fullertonhotel.com Tel: +65 6733 8388

Park Hyatt Tokyo – Page 88
3 – 7 – 1 – 2 Nishi – Shinjuku, Shinjuku – ku, Tokyo
Email: reservation.phtokyo@hyatt.com
www.tokyo.park.hyatt.com Tel: +81 3 5322 1234

Fullerton Bay Hotel – Page 74
80 Collyer Quay, 049326, Singapore
Email: info@fullertonbayhotel.com
www.fullertonbayhotel.com Tel: +65 6333 8388

The Lodge at Tarraleah – Page 89
Wild River Road, Tarraleah, Tasmania, 7140
Email: info@tarraleahlodge.com
www.tarraleahlodge.com Tel: +61 3 6289 1199

Amankila – Page 76
Manggis, Bali, Indonesia
Email: amankila@amanresorts.com
www.amanresorts.com Tel: +65 363 41333

Wolgan Valley Resort & Spa – Page 90
2600 Wolgan Road, Wolgan Valley, Lithgow, NSW27
Email: reservations@wolganvalley.com
www.wolganvalley.com Tel: +61 2 6350 1800

Ayana Resort & Spa – Page 77
Ji. Karang Mas Sejahtera, Jimbaran, Bali
Email: reservation@ayanresort.com
www.ayanaresort.com Tel: +62 – 361 – 702222

Huka Lodge – Page 92
271 Huka Falls Road, Taupo, 3377
Email: reservation@hukalodge.co.nz
www.hukalodge.co.nz Tel: + 64 7 378 5791

China World Summit Wing – Page 78
1 Jianguomenwai Avenue, Chaoyang District, Beijing
Email: reservations.cwsw@shangri-la.com
www.shangri-la.com Tel: +86 10 65050 2299

Eagles Nest – Page 93
60 Tapeka Road, Russell, Bay of Islands
Email: eagle@eaglesnest.co.nz
www.eaglesnest.co.nz Tel: +64 9403 8333

Aman at Summer Palace – Page 79
1 Gongmenqian Street, Summer Palace, Beijing
Email: amanatsummerpalace@amanresorts.com
www.amanresorts.com Tel: +86 10 5987 9999

EUROPE

Hotel D'Angleterre – Page 96
Kongens Nytorv 34, Copenhagen, 1050
Email: room@dangleterre.dk
www.dangleterre.com Tel: +45 33 37 06 55

Homa Chateau – Page 80
Dabu Town, Guilin, Yanshan District
Email: guilinhoma@yuzile.com
www.guilinhoma.com Tel: +86 773 386 9066

Aldourie Castle Estate – Page 97
Loch Ness, Inverness
Email: info@aldouriecastle.co.uk
www.aldouriecastle.co.uk Tel: +44 870 625 0265

The Peninsula Hong Kong – Page 82
Salisbury Road, Kowloon, Hong Kong
Email: phk@peninsula.com
www.hongkong.peninsula.com Tel: +852 2920 2888

Alladale Wilderness Lodge & Resort – Page 98
Ardgay, Sutherland, IV24 3BS, Scotland
Email: enquiries@alladale.com
www.alladale.com Tel: +44 1863 755 338

W Hong Kong – Page 84
1 Austin Road West, Kowloon Station, Kowloon, Hong Kong
Email: w.hk@whotels.com
www.whotels.com/hongkong Tel: +852 3717 2222

Lismore Castle – Page 99
Lismore, County Waterford, Ireland
Email: info@lismorecastle.com
www.lismorecastle.com Tel: +353 (0)58 54288

Island Shangri-La – Page 86
Supreme Court Road, Pacific Palace, Central
Email: reservations.isl@shangri-la.com
www.shangri-la.com Tel: +852 2820 8333

The Grove – Page 100
Chandlers Cross, Hertfordshire, WD3 4TG
Email: info@thegrove.co.uk
www.thegrove.co.uk Tel: +44 (0) 1923 807807

Hotel Endsleigh – Page 101
Milton Abbot, Tavistock, Devon, England
Email: mail@hotelendsleigh.com
www.hotelendsleigh.com Tel: +44 1822 870 000

Le Royal Monceau, Raffles Paris – Page 116
37 Avenue Hoche, Paris, 75008
Email: paris.sales@raffles.com
www.leroyalmonceau.com Tel: +331 42 998800

The Dorchester – Page 102
53 Park Lane, London, England
Email: info@thedorchester.com
www.thedorchester.com Tel: +44 207 629 8888

La Réserve Paris Apartments – Page 117
3 Avenue D'Eylau, Paris, 75116
Email: info@lareserve-paris.com
www.lareserve-paris.com Tel: +33 1 53 70 53 70

Claridge's – Page 104
Brook Street, Mayfair, London, W1K 4HR
Email: info@claridges.com
www.claridges.co.uk Tel: +44 20 7629 8860

La Réserve Ramatuelle Hotel Spa& Villas – Page 118
Chemin de la Quessine, Ramatuelle, 83350
Email: info@lareserve-ramatuelle.com
www.lareserve-ramatuelle.com Tel: +33 494 44 94 44

The Savoy – Page 105
Strand, London, WC2R 0EU
Email: savoy@fairmont.com
www.fairmont.com/savoy Tel: +44 20 7836 4343

Le Negresco – Page 120
37 Promenade des Anglais, Nice, France
Email: info@hotel-negresco.com
www.hotel-negresco-nice.com Tel: +33 4 93 16 64 00

The Athenaeum – Page 106
116 Piccadilly, Mayfair, London
Email: info@athenaeumhotel.com
www.athenaeumhotel.com Tel: +44 20 7499 3464

Chateau de Bagnols – Page 121
Le Bourg, Bagnols, 69620
Email: info@chateaudebagnols.fr
www.chateaudebagnols.fr Tel: +33 4 74 71 40 00

Brown's Hotel – Page 107
Albemarle Street, Mayfair, London
Email: reservations.browns@roccofortecollection.com
www.brownshotel.com Tel: +44 20 7493 6020

Gstaad Palace – Page 122
28 Palacestrasse, Gstaad, 3780
Email: info@palace.ch
www.palace.ch Tel: +41 337 485 890

The Halkin – page 108
Halkin Street, London, England
Email: res@halkin.como.bz
www.halkin.como.bz Tel: +44 20 333 1000

Beau-Rivage Palace – Page 123
17 – 19 Palace du Port, Lausanne 6, CH – 1000
Email: reservation@brp.ch
www.brp.ch Tel: +41 21613 33 33

Grand-Hotel du Cap-Ferrat – Page 110
71 Boulevard du General de Gaulle,
Saint-Jean Cap-Ferrat, France
Email: reserv@grand-hotel-cap-ferrat.com
www.grand-hotel-cap-ferrat.com Tel: +33 4 93 76 50 50

La Réserve Genève, Hotel and Spa – Page 124
301, route de Lausanne, Bellevue, 1293 CH
Email: info@lareserve.ch
www.lareserve.ch Tel: +41 229 59 59 59

Hotel Ritz Paris – Page 112
15 Place Vendome, Paris, France
Email: resa@ritzparis.com
www.ritzparis.com Tel: +33 143 16 30 30

Hotel des Trois Couronnes – Page 125
49 Rue d'Italie, Vevey, 1800
Email: info@hoteltroiscouronnes.ch
www.hoteltroiscouronnes.ch Tel: +41 21 923 32 00

Hotel Plaza Athénée Paris – Page 114
25 Avenue Montaigne, Paris, Region Parisienne, 75008
Email: reservations@plaza-athenee-paris.com
www.plaza-athenee-paris.com Tel: +33 1 53 67 66 65

Grand Hotel Les Trois Rois – Page 126
8 Blumenrain, Basel, 4001
Email: reservation@lestroisrois.com
www.lestroisrois.com Tel: +41 61 260 51 25

Hotel Le Meurice – Page 115
228 rue de Rivoli, Paris, France
Email: reservations@lemeurice.com
www.lemeurice.com Tel: +33 1 44 58 10 00

DO & CO Hotel Vienna – Page 127
12 Stephansplatz, Vienna, 1010
Email: hotel@doco.com
www.doco.com Tel: +43 1 24 188423

Elounda Bay Palace Hotel – Page 153
Elounda, Crete, 72053, Greece
Email: bay@eloundabay.gr
www.eloundabay.gr Tel: + 30 28410 67000

Gran Melia Resort & Luxury Villas Daios Cove – Page 154
Vathi, Aghios Nikolaos, Crete
Email: gran.melia.crete@solmelia.com
www.granmeliacrete.com Tel: +30 28410 62600

Nafplia Palace Hotel & Villas – Page 155
Akronafplia, 21100 Nafplion, Peloponnese
Email: reservationsfit@helioshotels.gr
www.nafpliapalace.gr Tel: +30 210 36 79 000

A'Jia Hotel – Page 156
Cubuklu Cad. No 27, Kanlica, Istanbul
Email: info@ajiahotel.com
www.ajiahotel.com Tel: +90 216 413 9300

Kempinski Hotel Barbaros Bay Bodrum – Page 157
Kizilagac Koyu, Gerenkuyu Mevkii, Yaliciftlik, Bodrum
Email: reservations.barbaros@kempinski.com
www.kempinski-bodrum.com Tel: +90 252 311 0303

The Sofa Hotel Nisantasi – Page 158
41 – 4 Tesvikiye Cad, A Nisantasi Sisli, Istanbul, 34367
Email: sekren@thesofahotel.com
www.thesofahotel.com Tel: +90212 3681818

Museum Hotel – Page 159
No.1 Tekelli Mah, Neveshir, Cappadocia, Uchisar
Email: info@museum-hotel.com
www.museum-hotel.com Tel: +90 384 219 2220

Rodina Grand Hotel & Spa – Page 160
33 Vinogradnaya Street, Sochi, Krasnodar Region
Email: info@grandhotelrodina.ru
www.grandhotelrodina.ru Tel: +7 8622 539 000

Ararat Park Hyatt Moscow – Page 161
4 Neglinnaya Street, Moscow, 109012
Email: moscow.park@hyatt.com
www.moscow.park.hyatt.com Tel: +7 495 783 1234

Sonora Resort – Page 164
12831 Horseshoe Place, Richmond BC, V7A 4X5
Email: info@sonoraresort.com
www.sonoraresort.com Tel: +1 604 – 233 – 0460

Fairmont Pacific Rim – Page 165
1038 Canada Place, Vancouver, British Columbia, V6C 0B9
Email: fairmont@pacificrim.com
www.fairmontpacificrim.com Tel: +1 604 781 4303

The Greenwich Hotel – Page 166
337 Greenwich Street, New York, NY10013
Email: reservations@thegreenwichhotel.com
www.thegreenwichhotel.com Tel: +1 212 941 8900

The Standard – Page 168
848 Washington Street at West 13th New York, NY 10014
Email: nyreservations@standardhotel.com
www.standardhotels.com Tel: +1 212 645 4646

The Mark – Page 169
Madison Avenue at 77th Street, New York, NY10075
Email: reservations@themarkhotel.com
www.themarkhotel.com Tel:m +1 212 744 4300

The Plaza Hotel – Page 170
Fifth Avenue at Central Park, New York, NY 10019
Email: plazareservation@fairmont.com
www.fairmont.com/theplaza Tel: +1 212 759 3000

Sanctuary Camelback Mountain Resort & Spa – Page 172
5700 E.McDonald Drive, Paradise Valley, AZ 85253
Email: info@sanctuaryaz.com
www.sanctuaryoncamelback.com Tel: +1 800 245 2051

Chateau Marmont – Page 174
8221 Sunset Boulevard, Los Angeles, CA 90046
Email: reservations@chateaumarmont.com
www.chateaumarmont.com Tel: +1 323 656 1010

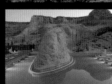

Amangiri – Page 175
1 Kayenta Road, Canyon Point, Utah
Email: amangiri@amanresorts.com
www.amanresorts.com Tel: +1 435 675 3999

Blantyre – Page 176
16 Balantyre Road, Lenox, MA 01240
Email: welcome@blantyre.com
www.blantyre.com Tel: +413 637 3556

XV Beacon Hotel – Page 177
15 Beacon Street, Boston, MA
Email: reservations@xvbeacon.com
www.xvbeacon.com Tel: +1 617 670 1500

Wynn Las Vegas & Encore – Page 178
3131 Las Vegas Boulevard, South Las Vegas, NV 89109
Email: roomreservations@wynnlasvegas.com
www.wynnlasvegas.com Tel: +1 702 770 7000

The Setai – Page 179
2001 Collins Avenue, South Beach, Miami Beach
Email: setai@ghmamericas.com
www.setai.com Tel: +1 305 520 6000

Delano – Page 180
1685 Collins Avenue, Miami Beach, Florida
Email: info@delano – hotel.com
www.delano – hotel.com Tel: +1 305 672 2000

Mondrian – Page 181
1100 West Avenue, Miami Beach, Florida, 33139
Email: info@mondrian.com
www.mondrian-miami.com Tel: +1 305 514 1500

Las Ventanas al Paraiso, A Rosewood Resort – Page 182
KM 19.5 Ctra. Transpeninsular, San Jose del
Cabo, Baja California Sur, 23400
Email: lasventanas@rosewoodhotels.com
www.lasventanas.com Tel: +1 52 624 144 2800

Nandana Private Resort – Page 183
Nandana Private Resort, Pine Island, Grand Bahama
Email: info@nandanaresort.com
www.nandanaresort.com Tel: +877 220 0737

Necker Island – Page 184
Necker Island, Virgin Gorda, British Virgin Islands
Email: info@neckerisland.com
www.neckerisland.com Tel: +1 800 716 919

Eden Rock – St. Barths – Page 185
Baie de St. Jean, St. Barths, French West Indies, 97133
Email: info@edenrockhotel.com
www.edenrockhotel.com Tel: +590 590 29 79 99

Isle De France – Page 186
Hotel St Barth Isle de France, Hotel St Barth Isle
de France B.P. 612, Baie des Flamands
Email: hotel@isle – de – france.com
www.isle-de-france.com Tel: +59 0590 276181

Como Shambhala at Parrot Cay – Page 187
Como Shambhala, Providenciales, Turks & Caicos Islands
Email: res@parrotcay.como.bz
www.parrotcay.como.bz Tel: +1 649 946 7788

Viceroy Anguilla – Page 188
Barnes Bay, West End, AI – 2640
Email: concierge@viceroyanguilla.com
www.viceroyanguilla.com Tel: +1 264 497 7000

Ponta dos Ganchos Exclusive Resort – Page 190
104 Rua Eupidio Alves do Nascimento,
Governador Celso Ramos, Santa Catarina
Email: reservation@pontadosganchos.com.br
www.pontadosganchos.com.br Tel: +55 48 39537000

Hotel Unique – Page 191
4.700 Av.Brigadeiro Luis Antonio, Jardim Paulistano, Sao Paulo
Email: reservas@hotelunique.com.br
www.hotelunique.com.br Tel: +55 11 3055 4710

Hotel Fasano São Paulo – Page 192
Vittorio Fasano 88, São Paulo, 01414020
Email: sp@fasano.com.br
www.fasano.com.br Tel: +55 11 3896 4077

Hotel Fasano Rio de Janeiro– Page 193
Av. Vieira Souto 80, Rio de Janeiro, 22420 000
Email: rio@fasano.com.br
www.fasano.com.br Tel: +55 11 3896 4108

Pousada Picinguaba – Page 194
Ubatuba, São Paulo, Brazil
Email: info@picinguaba.com
www.picinguaba.com Tel: +55 12 3836 9103

Faena Hotel & Universe – Page 195
445 Martha Salotti, Buenos Aires, Argentina
Email: reservations@faenaexperience.com
www.faenahotelanduniverse.com Tel: +54 4010 9000

Llao Llao Hotel & Resort, Golf-Spa – Page 196
25 Av. Ezequiel Bustillo, Bariloche, Rio Negro
Email: reservations@llaollao.com.ar
www.llaollao.com Tel: +54 2944 448530

Hotel de Larache – Page 197
Domingo de Atienza S/N, San Pedro de Atacama, II Region
Email: atacama@explora.com
www.explora.com Tel: +56 2 395 2800

Explora Patagonia – Page 198
Casilla 57, Puerto Natales, Chile
Email@ patagonia@explora.com
www.explora.com/patagonia Tel: +1 866 750 6699

Indigo Patagonia Hotel & Spa – Page 199
Ladrilleros 105, Puerto Natales, Chile
Email: info@indigopatagonia.com
www.indigopatagonia.com Tel: +56 61 413 609

QUINTESSENTIALLY TV
IS A FILM PRODUCTION COMPANY

WE CREATE BESPOKE HIGH QUALITY VIDEOS FOR
BRANDS AND COMPANIES, FROM CORPORATE
AND PROMOTIONAL FILMS TO EDITORIAL AND
ADVERTORIAL CONTENT.

VIDEO IS THE MOST FLEXIBLE FORM OF COMMUNICATION
AND CAN BE PLACED ON

- WEBSITES INCLUDING SOCIAL MEDIA CHANNELS
- VIDEO BANNERS AND VIRAL ADVERTS
- ONLINE TV CHANNELS
- BROADCAST CHANNELS
- CONFERENCE AND INTERNAL TV SCREENS
- DVDs
- LINKS IN EMAIL SIGNATURES AND NEWSLETTERS

Video has a positive impact on clients by increasing brand awareness
and therefore driving sales as well as creating potential leads for
new business.

Video campaigns are more durable, their success can be tracked
and they can be re-edited and updated for different projects and
promotions.

To find out how video can support you or for a free project consultation
please contact us at contactqtv@quintessentially.com
0202 292 5113

www.quintessentiallytv.com

QUINTESSENTIALLY TV

QUINTESSENTIALLY NATURAL

Quintessentially Natural is the purest water known to the world and is sourced from the North Western Point of Tasmania, an area recognised for possessing the cleanest air on earth.

The water is not exposed to contamination as it is collected before it reaches the ground and is bottled at source. Quintessentially Natural is only available to Quintessentially members and a few select distributors.

www.quintessentiallynatural.com
info@quintessentiallynatural.com

ACKNOWL■■GM■NT■

We have thoroughly enjoyed compiling this edition of Quintessentially Reserve. We are very proud of the featured properties in this year's title and its slick and fresh look. The future looks bright for Quintessentially Publishing, and its team of dedicated and talented experts make it the vibrant company it is today. So it is with gratitude and pride that thanks and admiration must go to Lois Crompton for her determination and personable way no matter how hard the task of production, Barry Lynch, Chloe Street, Nathalie Grainger, Lana Elie, Bonnie Silver, Gemma Silver and Will Sutton for their hard work and faith, and Chris Rayner and Edward Rodwell for managing the entire project of this book with belief and energy. Thanks are also due to the entire Quintessentially Design team and in particular Marjus Burokas for diligence and skill, Leanne Simpson for guidance and vision. Finally, to the Quintessentially global team for their knowledge and support throughout all stages of production of this book.